TIME
Nature's Extremes

MONTANA, 2000 *Two elk take refuge in the East Fork of the Bitterroot River as a wildfire, an essential part of the natural process, rages across the hills*

TIME

MANAGING EDITOR Richard Stengel
ART DIRECTOR D.W. Pine

Nature's Extremes

Earthquakes, Tsunamis and the Other Natural Disasters
That Shape Life on Earth

EDITOR Kelly Knauer
DESIGNER Ellen Fanning
PICTURE EDITOR Patricia Cadley
RESEARCH Tresa McBee; Matthew McCann Fenton
ORIGINAL GRAPHICS Lon Tweeten
COPY EDITOR Bruce Christopher Carr

TIME HOME ENTERTAINMENT
PUBLISHER Richard Fraiman
GENERAL MANAGER Steven Sandonato
EXECUTIVE DIRECTOR, MARKETING SERVICES Carol Pittard
EXECUTIVE DIRECTOR, RETAIL & SPECIAL SALES Tom Mifsud
EXECUTIVE DIRECTOR, NEW PRODUCT DEVELOPMENT Peter Harper
DIRECTOR, BOOKAZINE DEVELOPMENT & MARKETING Laura Adam
PUBLISHING DIRECTOR Joy Butts
ASSISTANT GENERAL COUNSEL Helen Wan
BOOK PRODUCTION MANAGER Suzanne Janso
DESIGN & PREPRESS MANAGER Anne-Michelle Gallero
BRAND MANAGER Michela Wilde
ASSOCIATE PREPRESS MANAGER Alex Voznesenskiy

SPECIAL THANKS
Christine Austin, Jeremy Biloon, Glenn Buonocore, Malati Chavali, Jim Childs, Susan
Chodakiewicz, Rose Cirrincione, Brian Fellows, Jacqueline Fitzgerald, Christine Font, Carrie
Frazier, Lauren Hall, Mona Li, Robert Marasco, Kimberly Marshall, Amy Migliaccio, Nina Mistry,
Dave Rozzelle, Ilene Schreider, Adriana Tierno, Jonathan White, Vanessa Wu, TIME Imaging

We welcome your comments and suggestions about TIME Books. Please write to us at:
TIME Books, Attention: Book Editors, PO Box 11016, Des Moines, IA 50336-1016

If you would like to order any of our hardcover Collector's Edition books, please call us at
1-800-327-6388, Monday–Friday, 7 a.m.–8 p.m., or Saturday, 7 a.m.–6 p.m., Central Time.

**A portion of the proceeds from this volume will be donated to relief efforts for the
March 11, 2011, earthquake and tsunami in Japan.**

URI GOLMAN—NPL—MINDEN PICTURES

ICELAND, 2010 *The eruption of the island nation's Eyjafjallajokull volcano shut down airline travel in Europe for more than a week*

Contents

MULVANE, KANSAS, 2004 *Nature's might and beauty join forces as a roaring tornado crosses the path of a rainbow*

The Day the Earth Moved

By Nancy Gibbs

THE 9.0 QUAKE THAT HIT JAPAN ON March 11 was powerful enough to shift the earth on its axis and make the planet spin a little faster, shortening the day by 1.8 millionths of a second. It shoved the island nation one parking space to the east. But what felt like the end was just the beginning.

The sturdy buildings that survived the quake were ravaged by the waves that followed. The three-story walls of water dissolved coastal towns, dry-docked boats on the roofs of buildings and shuffled houses like playing cards. There were so many aftershocks that people stopped diving under tables. Those who made it safely to higher ground waited in the dark, in the cold, in lines that stretched for hours for water and food. In a society seen as the most stoic on Earth, the closest thing to chaos was a man cutting in line.

But still it was not over; only the earth and sea had spoken. The next danger came from the sky. Officials warned people to stay inside and seal whatever was left of their homes because the new threat was silent, invisible—and airborne. A rich country perched on four fault lines and with no oil reserves embraces nuclear power with the caution born of long memory and scars. But no one calculated what would happen if the fail-safes failed.

When the quake hit, the reactors at the Fukushima Daiichi complex did exactly what they were supposed to do: they shut down. But then the wave came, breached the seawall, drowned the backup generators needed to cool the reactors and took out the spare batteries. It was left to a skeleton crew of 50 to jury-rig fire hoses to keep the temperatures down.

One by one, the outer buildings exploded. This is also what they were designed to do, to release pressure and protect the core. The best nuclear scientists on the planet raced to avert a total meltdown even as radioactivity levels as far south as Tokyo spiked to 23 times as high as normal. With the menace growing by the hour, the most fateful calculation came down to the most fickle: Which way is the wind blowing?

It only started as a natural disaster; the next waves were all man-made, as money fled to higher ground. Fear and uncertainty sheared $700 billion off the Toyko Stock Exchange in three days. Japan makes nearly a quarter of the world's semiconductors and most of its gadgets. Sony suspended production at seven plants; carmakers slowed output, fearful of gaps in the supply chain; power companies scheduled rolling blackouts. How can a global recovery take hold if the world's third largest economy is out of business, even temporarily? Meanwhile, Switzerland announced a freeze on new nuclear plants, Germany shut down all its facilities built before 1980, and the U.S. Congress called for hearings on nuclear safety. The flooded Japanese plant will never reopen. But demand for power only grows.

We sleep easy in the soft arms of clichés: hope for the best, prepare for the worst; risk varies inversely with knowledge; it's a waste of time to think about the unthinkable. But Japan shook those soothing assumptions. No amount of planning, no skills or specs or spreadsheets, can stop a force that moves the planet. ■

JAPANESE ARCHIPELAGO *The islands that make up the nation in the Pacific Ocean were photographed from space in 1999 by a NASA satellite designed to study Earth's climate*

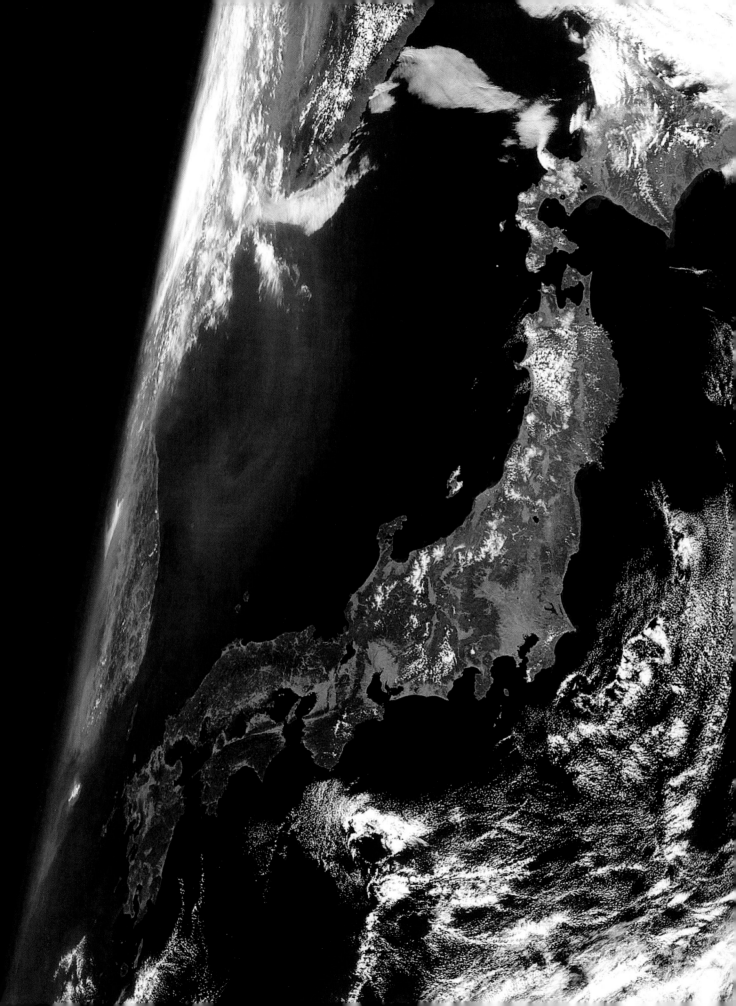

OARAI CITY, JAPAN, 2011 *When the largest earthquake in the nation's recorded history struck some 80 miles (129 km) off the eastern shores of the archipelago on March 11, it triggered massive tsunami waves that devastated coastal towns and left this whirlpool hovering offshore from the town in Ibaraki prefecture*

RESTLESS PLANET

Our planet is unsettled, unruly, a work in progress. And it follows its own agenda, in which human beings play a minor role. When tectonic plates move and an earthquake occurs, as it did off the northeast coast of Japan in March 2011, millions of human lives can be profoundly altered within hours and days. Deadly events—tornadoes and hurricanes, volcanic eruptions and wildfires—are driven by natural forces that we are still struggling to understand and predict, and cannot yet dream of controlling.

Enter the Tsunami

NATORI, JAPAN, 2011 When the waves generated by the March 11 earthquake off the nation's coast reached this city in Miyagi prefecture, they battered trees and houses along the shore. The 9.0-magnitude quake was far stronger than seismologists had predicted would ever strike in this area, and the coastal town's seawalls were easily topped by the incoming waves. As of the end of March, authorities said that more than 11,000 people were dead and 17,000 were still missing, with the death toll expected to keep rising.

The Seekers

OTSUCHI, JAPAN, 2011 Rescue workers search for survivors amid the mind-boggling devastation wrought by the tsunami on this town in Iwate prefecture. Otsuchi was particularly hard-hit by the big waves: officials said that of the town's 16,000 residents, almost 1,000 had died, including the mayor and eight other officials, and some 6,000 were left homeless. (In Japan's samurai tradition, the word *otsuchi* refers to a long, wooden-handled hammer used by warriors to break down the gates and doors of fortified castles.)

ALY SONG / REUTERS / CORBIS

Fish Out of Water

HACHINOHE, JAPAN, 2011 The tsunami waves generated by the magnitude-9.0 earthquake that struck in the Pacific Ocean off the coasts of the Japanese archipelago were so powerful as to defy everyday constants of gravity and weight. In this coastal city of some 240,000 residents in the Aomori prefecture, the waves left a fishing trawler lying on its side in a downtown street. But the city was not so devastated as some of its neighbors; "only" some 100 homes were destroyed when the ocean waves roared through.

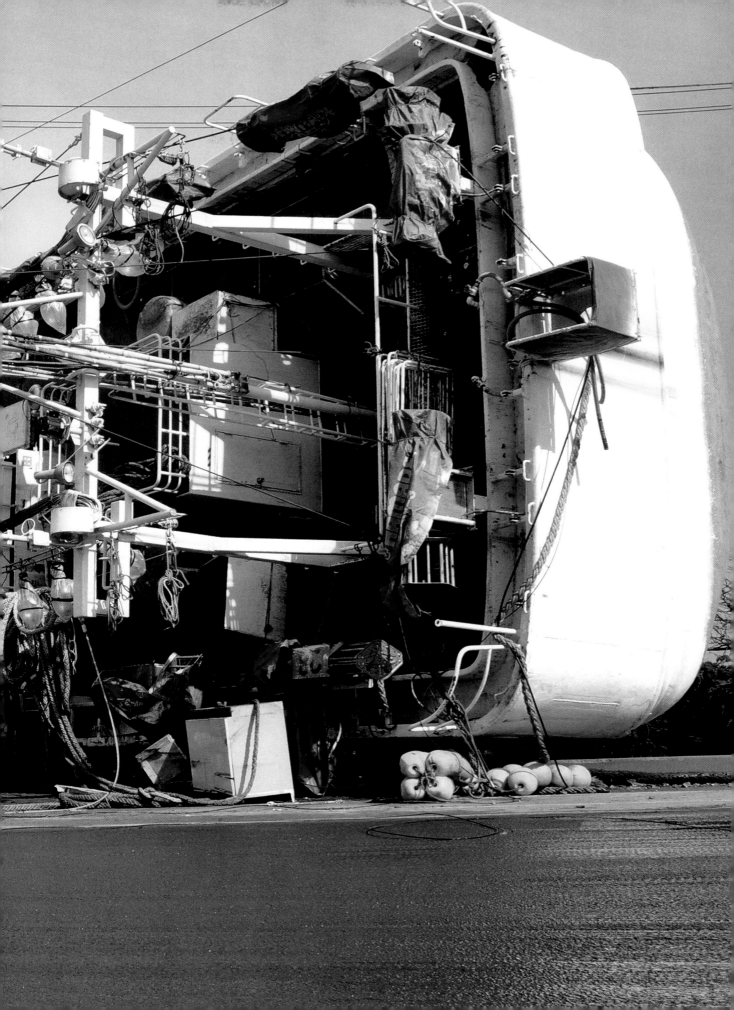

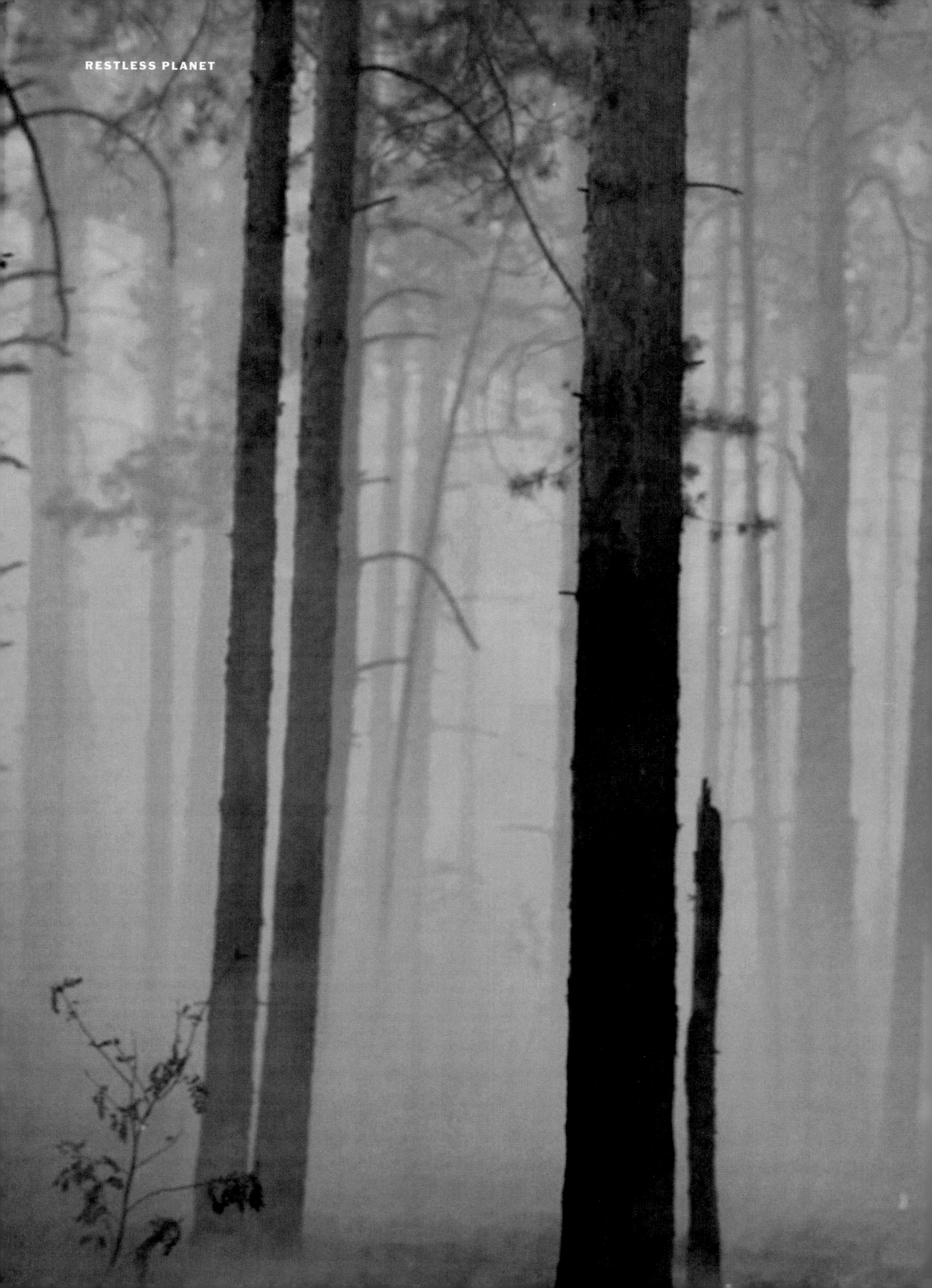

Wildfires Breed a Toxic Haze

GOLOVANOVO, RUSSIA, 2010 Civilian firefighters, outmatched by the forces they are struggling to control, battle flames in the village in the Ryazan Oblast as Russia faced the largest outbreak of wildfires in recorded history. In July and August, hundreds of fires raged across the central and western regions of the vast nation, creating a toxic cloud of smog that hovered over Moscow and other cities for weeks. More than 50,000 people, many already suffering from respiratory ailments, died before the fires were controlled and the smog lifted.

An Earthquake Devastates Haiti

PORT-AU-PRINCE, 2010 At 4:53 p.m. on Tuesday, Jan. 12, a magnitude-7.0 quake rocked the island nation, radiating outward from the town of Leogane, some 16 miles (25 km) west of the capital city. But that was close enough: the big temblor demolished Port-au-Prince and plunged the already impoverished nation into survival mode. More than a year after the event, estimates of the total dead still varied widely, though most sources believe in excess of 200,000 people died at the least, and 1 million others were left homeless.

Something in the Air

EYJAFJALLAJOKULL, ICELAND, 2010 The town's eponymous volcano had been relatively quiet since 1821-23, but the big cone became active in March, then went silent until April 14, when a major eruption began. As it belched huge clouds of ash into the sky, local ranchers drove their horses away from the area. This relatively minor incident claimed no lives and might have passed without the world's notice—except the volcano's cloud of grit and ash shut down airline flights all across Europe for six days in April, inconveniencing millions.

Atlas Swallowed

GUATEMALA CITY, 2007 Few things seem as substantial as the solid ground beneath our feet, but in some places the ground is far from firm. Guatemala's capital city is built upon a slim layer of pyroclastic ash, matter expelled from a volcano that cools down to form land but which remains permeable. This crater appeared on Feb. 26 after a sewer line ruptured; at 330 ft. (100 m) deep, it was the size of a 30-story building. It swallowed a dozen homes and killed three people. A similar sinkhole opened on May 30, 2010, but no one died.

A Matter of Gravity

NOVA FRIBURGO, BRAZIL, 2011 After heavy rains soaked Rio de Janeiro state during January (summer in the southern hemisphere), gigantic mudslides in three towns of the hilly region—Nova Friburgo, Petrópolis and Teresópolis—claimed at least 600 lives and left some 14,000 people homeless. It was the deadliest single natural disaster in the history of Brazil, which has never suffered a major hurricane, earthquake or volcanic eruption. But as the global climate heats up, flooding and mudslides are more common in the nation.

The processes that drive our planet's constant changes are so vast as to challenge our comprehension. Can it be that the solid ground under our feet isn't always solid? Yes, for earthquake survivors report seeing the landscape around them churning like the waves of the ocean. Can it be that the interior of our world is composed of two intensely hot cores, one liquid and one solid? Yes, for we receive occasional postcards from the planet's interior in the form of the molten lava expelled by volcanoes. Can it be that the continents of the globe slowly move, as the giant tectonic plates they rest upon grind against one another? Yes, for it is precisely at these seams in the skin of the planet that we see the potent proof of its dynamics—as deadly natural disasters in Japan and New Zealand in 2011 reminded us.

INSIDE
THE
PLANET

KLIUCHEVSKOI VOLCANO, KAMCHATKA, RUSSIA, 1994 *A space shuttle camera took this false-color radar image of the volcano erupting (blue and white areas). The red areas are snow cover*

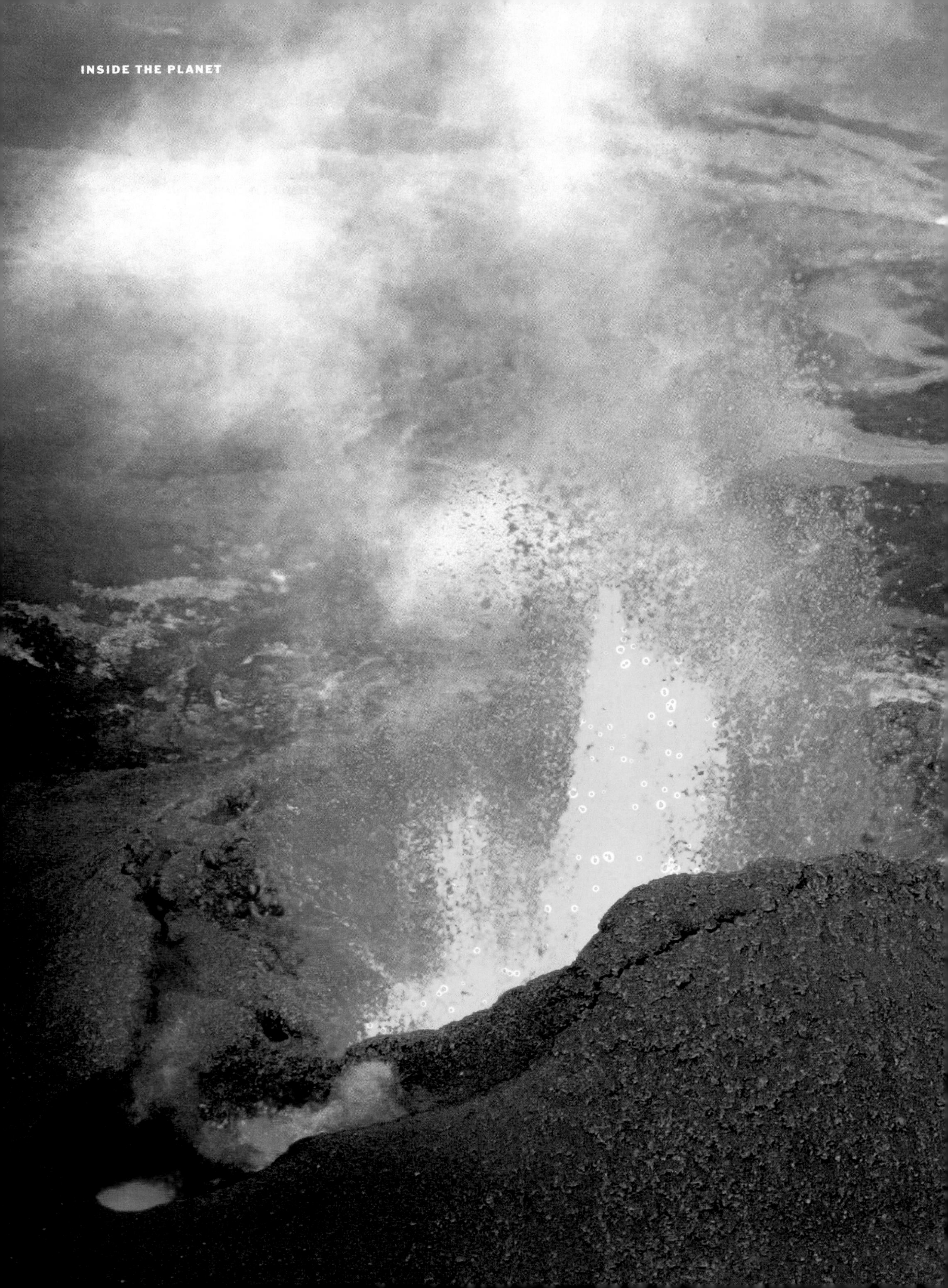

A Furnace That Forges Land

PITON DE LA FOURNAISE, REUNION ISLAND Among the liveliest of the world's active volcanoes, Piton de la Fournaise is one of two belching behemoths that formed this island in the western Indian Ocean; here it is seen erupting on Nov. 16, 2002. More than 8,000 ft. (2,400 m) high, Réunion's "Furnace Peak" has erupted more than 150 times since 1640, steadily enlarging the island, which is some 950 sq. mi. in extent and home to more than 700,000 people. The volcano erupted twice in 2010.

Where Continents Collide

OEFAERUFOSS WATERFALL, ELDGJA CHASM, ICELAND Earth's surface consists of giant plates that support the continents and oceans. The discovery that these plates move, slowly floating atop the hot mantle below them, is the foundation of modern geoscience. They converge in a series of junctions that crisscross the planet's surface like the seams of a base-ball. The Eldgja Valley in Iceland is one of the most prominent of these convergence zones; others include the Great Rift Valley of eastern Africa and California's San Andreas Fault.

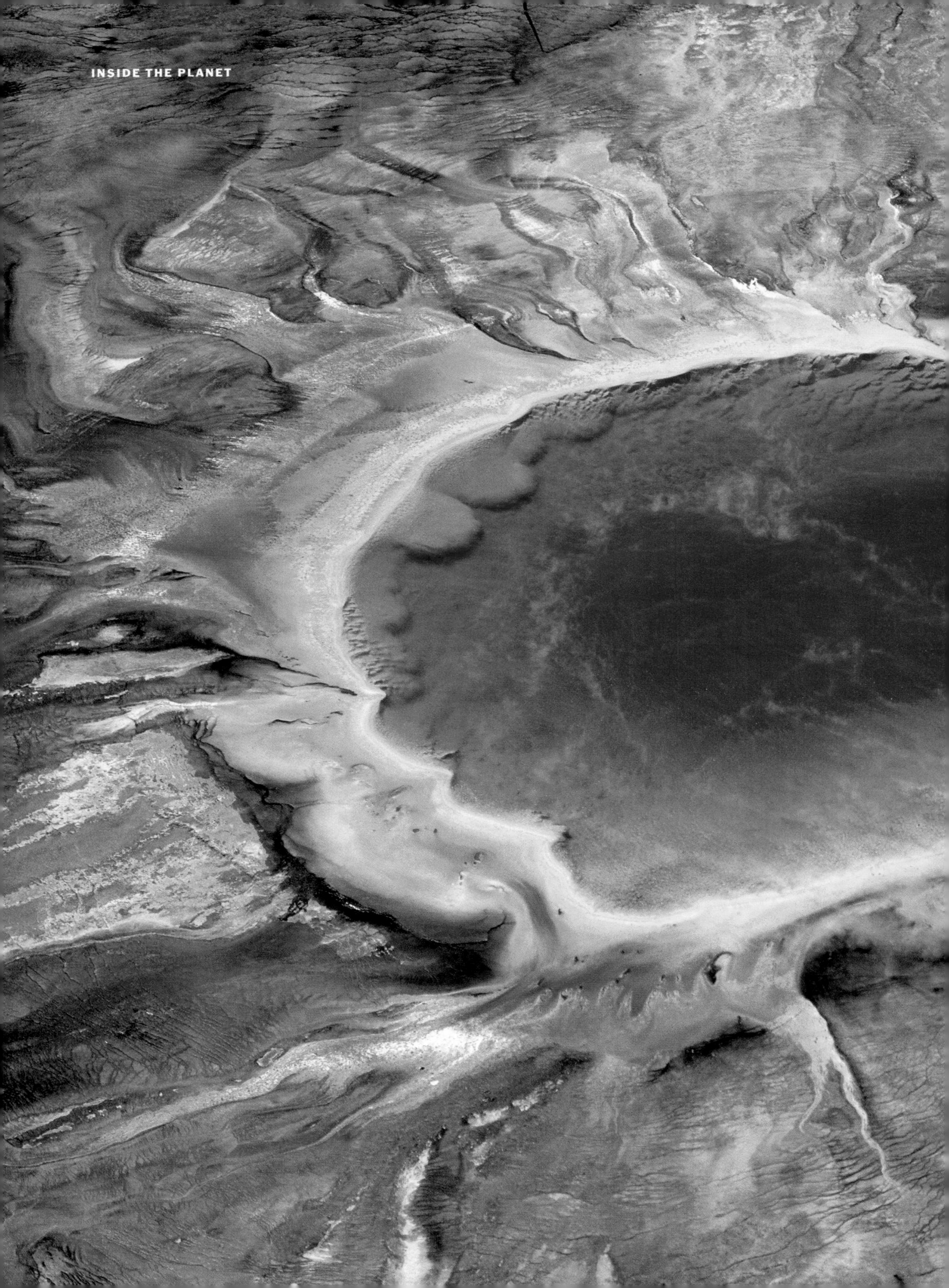

A Hot Liquid Rainbow

GRAND PRISMATIC SPRING, YELLOWSTONE NATIONAL PARK, WYOMING A large reservoir of hot magma lies not far below the ground in Yellowstone Park, cooking up a colorful array of geysers and hot springs. At 300 ft. (91 m) across and 160 ft. (49 m) deep, the Grand Prismatic Spring is the largest of the hot springs; viewers on a walkway provide a sense of its scale. At its deepest point, the water here is some 188°F (86°C). Bacteria and algae in the cooler water along the pool's edges produce pigments as a natural reaction to the sun.

BIG ONE–IN–WAITING
California's San Andreas Fault cleaves the Golden State in two, running from north of San Francisco, past Los Angeles and nearly to Mexico

Dance of The Land

The theory of plate tectonics is a planetary operating manual

STRANGE AS IT MAY SEEM," PHYSICIST Richard Feynman wrote in his 1985 book, *Six Easy Pieces,* "we understand the distribution of matter in the interior of the sun far better than we understand the interior of the earth." That curious neglect of the world beneath our feet in favor of the cosmos beyond may be hard-wired into our DNA. We are an exploring species, and the things truly worth exploring always seem to be *up there* rather than *down there.*

Need proof? Consider that while we've gazed at the stars and speculated about their origins for millennia, we didn't even realize that the Earth wasn't flat until 500 years ago, or one-tenth of 1% of human history. Indeed, human beings have been able to fly machines above the ground for longer than we have had an inkling that there is anything below that ground other than solid rock. Even in the geography of mythology, people of widely different cultures have always believed instinctively that the skies belong to the gods, and the realms beneath the ground are the domain of darker forces. After all, tidings from the Underworld—arriving chiefly in the form of hot lava or unsettling tremors—were almost invariably bad.

It was the search for worldly riches—gold , diamonds, oil and coal—that first prompted people to probe ever so slightly beneath the surface of our planet. What they found, usually a layer of soil or sand followed by solid rock, was assumed until the 20th century to represent the entire nature of the earth's interior. But in the past 100 years, humanity's knowledge of the world that lies beneath the surface has increased considerably, thanks to a handful of visionary scientists. Today we understand that many of the seemingly disparate natural disasters treated in this book—earthquakes and volcanoes, landslides and tsunamis—are all linked, each phenomenon the reflection of a planetary architecture whose forces are great enough to move continents, raise mountain ranges and drain oceans dry.

The scientist who revolutionized our view of geology was a German meteorologist, Alfred Wegener, who was only 30 when he wrote to his fiancé in 1910: "Doesn't the east coast of South America fit exactly against the west coast of Africa, as if they had once been joined? This is an idea I'll have to pursue." And he did just that, researching geologic and fossil records in university libraries all over Europe.

Some of Wegener's findings amazed him: remains of *Cynognathus,* a 9-ft.- (2.7 m-) long Triassic-era land reptile, had been discovered in two narrow strips of land, one in South America, the other in central Africa. When these continents were fitted together like jigsaw pieces, the two strips lined up perfectly. Another set of bands, in which fossils of the freshwater reptile *Mesosaurus* had been found, seemed to connect seamlessly across the lower latitudes of South America and Africa. A third dinosaur, *Lystrosaurus,* was found only in three strips traversing Africa, India and Antarctica, and these bands formed a single brushstroke when the shapes of those continents were linked.

For Wegener, the conclusion was clear, if mind-boggling: all the world's continents had once been joined in a single landmass, which he called Pangea, Greek for "All Earth." That giant landmass, he posited, had gradually broken apart, in a process he called "continental drift." Of course, the fossil evidence that Wegener used to support his theory had not gone unnoticed by other scientists. Yet in an example of how tenaciously mainstream scholars will cling to orthodoxy, geologists and paleontologists had explained these anomalies by hypothesizing a series of "land bridges," causeways that once linked continents across the world's oceans. The fact that there was little evidence, aside from a few well-known examples, that such bridges had ever existed seemed to bother no one.

What did bother nearly everyone, though, was the prospect that a young outsider—a mere weatherman, no less!—could upend the finely wrought theory of land bridges. "Utter, damned rot!" howled the president of the American Philosophical Society. Any person who "valued his reputation for scientific sanity" would dismiss such a theory out of hand, agreed a leading British geologist. When Wegener died, on an expedition to

PANGEA: ONE WORLD

All the planet's landmasses were once concentrated in a single supercontinent, Pangea (Greek for "whole earth"), which began breaking up around 225 million years ago

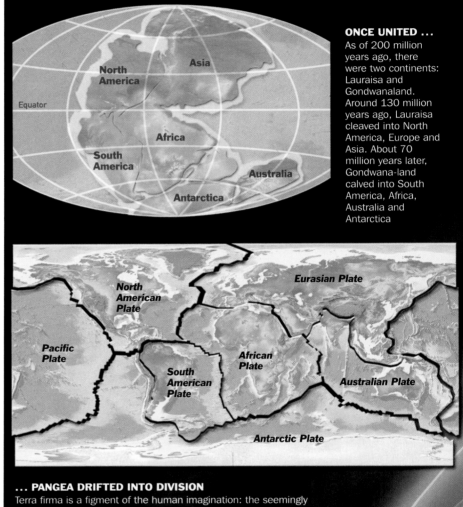

ONCE UNITED ...
As of 200 million years ago, there were two continents: Lauraisa and Gondwanaland. Around 130 million years ago, Lauraisa cleaved into North America, Europe and Asia. About 70 million years later, Gondwana-land calved into South America, Africa, Australia and Antarctica

... PANGEA DRIFTED INTO DIVISION
Terra firma is a figment of the human imagination: the seemingly solid surface of the earth is made up of more than a dozen vast plates floating above the liquid rock of the planet's interior and butting up against one another at tectonic convergence zones

PLANET EARTH: THE INSIDE STORY

The most solid part of our planet is right beneath your feet: go deeper than 50 miles, and the rock gets as soft as Silly Putty

The earth's interior resembles a soft-boiled egg with a hard outer crust, a soft layer of semisolid material underneath and hot liquid at the core

Crust
No more than 50 miles deep, this is the only part of the planet humans have seen

Upper Mantle
Not-so-solid rock, softened by heat from the planet's interior to the consistency of clay

Inner Core
A ball of iron and nickel, believed by some scientists to be hotter than the surface of the sun, it is kept solid by the stupendous pressure around it

Lower Mantle
Liquefied rock; this is the forge that supplies new land in the form of magma ejected from volcanoes

Outer Core
This sphere of liquid metal, mostly iron and nickel, spins with the planet's rotation, giving it a magnetic field

Continental crust

Trench

Subducting plate

Oceanic crust

LITHOSPHERE

ASTHENOSPHERE

Where plates on the earth's surface collide, one is sometimes wedged over the other, forcing the second plate down into the planet's interior, in a process called subduction. The older rock is submerged deep below the surface, where extremely high temperatures melt it down, recycling it into newer stone that rises once again to the crust. The cycle takes hundreds of millions of years to complete

early version of sonar, and Hess ordered that the equipment always remain on, thus compiling thousands of detailed readings about the contours of the seafloor. Among his first discoveries was the Mid-Atlantic Ridge, a vast mountain range that bisects the ocean, reaching almost from pole to pole. Hess and his colleagues would later discover that this ridge is one small part of a global chain of mountain ranges, mostly undersea, that stretch around the earth like seams on a baseball, and that many of these ranges consist of extinct or currently active volcanoes.

Taking core samples from these volcanic ranges, the geologists found that the rocks on top of the mountains were relatively young, just a few million years old, whereas rocks found on the slopes were older by tens of millions of years, and stones recovered far from the peaks were geologic senior citizens, hundreds of millions of years old. Their conclusion: new rock was continually bubbling up from somewhere inside the earth and was being ejected and pushed outward in the form of volcanic lava all along this line of ridges. The planet's surface, they reasoned, is actually composed of a series of giant plates that are continually moving, bearing continents and seas with them.

Today scientists believe the earth's crust is made up of 11 major segments, vast and solid, along with about 20 much smaller pieces, that float on a layer of molten rock that has the consistency of Silly Putty. The plates are called tectonic, from the Greek root meaning "to build," because they are continually building and reshaping the planet's surface while constantly jostling against one another like rafts crowded into a small pond. Along the boundaries where they meet, earthquakes and volcanoes are especially common.

When tectonic plates collide, one of three things oc-

Greenland in 1930, his theory of continental drift commanded about the same level of academic respect that speculation about the Bermuda Triangle does today.

One reason Wegener could be ignored was that he offered no theory as to how or why continents could move, like plows in a field, through the apparently solid surface of the planet. The explanation would have to await Harry Hess, a Princeton geologist who served as the commanding officer of a naval transport during World War II. Hess's ship was equipped with an

curs: they push each other upward to form mountain ranges, like the Himalayas; they push each other downward, which is how ocean trenches are formed; or they grind against each other, creating regions of instability. The last is what is happening where the two largest plates in the world, the Pacific and the North American, meet. One line between these two pieces of the planet's jigsaw skin is the San Andreas Fault, which gashes California for more than 650 miles (1,046 km). The two plates are moving so inexorably in opposite directions that the state's late seismologist Bruce Bolt once quipped, "In 30 million years, Los Angeles will become a new suburb of San Francisco."

The next unknown: What lies under the plates? Exploration of this interior frontier began in 1936, when Danish scientist Inge Lehmann used seismographic readings to deduce that earth's center consists of two concentric cores: a 1,300-mile (2,092 km) -thick liquid outer core and a solid inner core about 750 miles (1,207 km) in diameter. Both sections are composed mostly of iron and nickel, and it is these two nested spheres (especially the liquid outer core, which spins with the earth's rotation) that give the planet its magnetic field.

Lehmann built on earlier seismograph readings indicating that surrounding the core is a "mantle" layer of rock, 1,800 miles (2,896 km) thick, that is softened by the heat from the outer core. The mantle begins immediately beneath the 20-to-50-mile- (33-to-80-km-) thick crust, the earth's outermost layer. The mantle is the source of new volcanic rock, which causes ocean floors to spread, continents to drift and tectonic plates to collide. It is also the destination for older rock that is sucked back into the deepest part of the mantle, closest to the hot core, where it is melted and in effect recycled into new rock that bubbles back toward the surface. In a cycle that takes hundreds of millions of years to complete, the reconstituted rock is then ejected back through the crust by volcanic activity.

Further confirmation of the planet's tectonic architecture came from deep beneath the sea. In 1977 a team of scientists operating the submersible *Alvin* near the Galápagos Islands some 1.8 miles (2.9 km) beneath the ocean's surface discovered hydrothermal vents on the ocean floor, where billowing flows of hot water were emerging from cracks in the seabed. Like geysers aboveground, hydrothermal vents occur when seawater seeps through fissures into the crust and is heated by hot reservoirs of magma to some 350°F to 750°F (176-399°C), until it bursts back up through the oceanic crust. (Water that hot would boil on land, but at

the extreme depths at which the vents are located, the pressure of the surrounding ocean water raises the boiling point.)

The hot water that pours up through the vents is rich in minerals; when it mingles with the cold seawater, the minerals separate, in a process known as precipitation. Then they crystallize, often forming a chimney-like structure that surrounds the vent. Reflecting the enormous power that creates them, chimneys can grow very quickly, up to 30 ft. (9 m) in 18 months. The vents that spout water most heavily laden with minerals appear deep black and have been dubbed "black smokers"; other vents are "white smokers."

Unique life-forms, including giant tube worms and spider crabs, were soon discovered, thriving near these smoking vents on the ocean floor. Unlike any other sea or land animals, they are sustained by energy that is not derived from the sun in some manner. Instead, they harbor within their bodies large aggregations of bacteria that sustain themselves by turning the mineral sulfides pouring from the vents into oxygen—in short, by chemosynthesis, rather than by photosynthesis. These bacteria, in turn, provide nutrition for their hosts.

Thanks to this ongoing cascade of discoveries, Wegener's bold hypothesis was largely accepted by scientists by the 1960s. But there is much to learn. Humans have walked on the moon and sent probes to Mars but have never ventured more than a few miles beneath the surface of their home planet. More than 25 years on, Feynman's ideas still ring true: If our world were an apple, we have yet to pierce its skin. ■

GRACE UNDER PRESSURE *Above, colorful tube worms flourish near hot vents more than two miles (3.2 km) under the sea, in a sunless world. At right, a black smoker at the bottom of the Mid-Atlantic Ridge, a tectonic convergence zone, billows with heated, mineral-rich, recycled seawater*

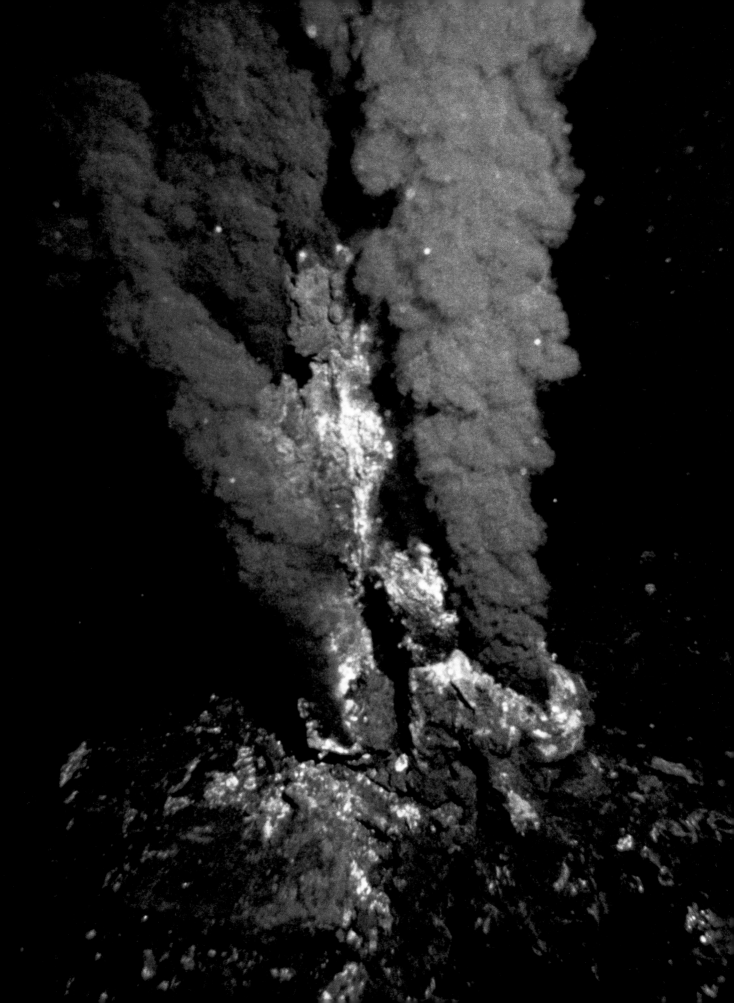

Cracks in the Crust

Earthquakes are among nature's deadliest killers. Can they be predicted?

TRAGEDY HAS A WAY OF VISITING THOSE who can bear it least. Haiti is the poorest nation in the western hemisphere, a place where malnutrition is widespread and less than half the population has access to clean drinking water. At 4:53 p.m. on Jan. 12, 2010, at a point 15 miles (24 km) southwest of the capital city, Port-au-Prince, the Caribbean tectonic plate pushed against the neighboring North American plate along a line known as the Enriquillo–Plantain Garden Fault system. On the earth's surface, the enormous energy created by the big tremor—an earthquake measuring 7.0 on the Richter scale—tossed the car that Bob Poff, the Salvation Army's director of disaster services in Haiti, was driving down the hill from the suburb of Pétionville to Port-au-Prince "to and fro like a toy." When the shaking stopped, Poff

HAITI, JANUARY 2010 *When the island nation was struck by a 7.0-magnitude earthquake, the city's buildings, many of them shoddy and poorly constructed, were leveled. Residents soon began the grim task of recovering the dead*

wrote on a Salvation Army blog, "I looked out of the windows to see buildings 'pancaking' down … Thousands of people poured into the streets, crying, carrying bloody bodies, looking for anyone who could help them."

Within the next few desperate hours, the scale of the catastrophe that had been unleashed upon Haiti became all too apparent. Twitter feeds and blog posts reported on the crisis in progress, asking if anyone had heard from loved ones, calling for medical supplies and Creole speakers. Louise Ivers, clinical director for Haiti for the NGO Partners in Health, wrote: "Port-au-Prince is devastated, lot of deaths. SOS. SOS … Please help us." Ian Rodgers of Save the Children posted, "We could hear buildings

still crumbling down five hours after the earthquake."

Three days later, TIME's Ioan Grillo reported from the stricken capital. "Like a thick fog, the stench of death curdles the air in the streets of this shattered city," he wrote. "It comes from trundling trucks, where corpses are piled up and covered by bloodstained sheets, while young men with scarves on their faces warn onlookers to stand aside. It is expelled from pyres of burning tires that incinerate cadavers that have remained unattended too long in the dust and heat, lit by residents afraid that the carrion will attract prowling dogs and endanger children. And it surges through piles of rocks and rubble, where hospitals, schools, palaces and homes fell like cards as the ground shook with the fiercest earthquake to strike this island in two centuries.

"The panorama of destruction appears endless. Street to street, neighborhood to neighborhood, ever more shattered buildings, wounded survivors and decaying corpses can be found. In one alley, two bodies lie across from a group of teenagers sitting and chatting. Around the corner, dozens of cadavers are piled in the remnants of a government building that reportedly had 1,000 employees. Photographer Shaul Schwarz, on assignment for TIME, saw corpses piled on the street impeding traffic ... No one can tell how many have perished, and the exact number of dead will be almost certainly never be known ... Tens of thousands? Hundreds of thousands?"

Unfortunately, Grillo's prediction was correct: as of late March 2011, estimates of the exact number of dead and missing after the big quake remained just that—estimates—and the numbers varied widely, ranging from a low of 92,000 dead and 1 million homeless to a high of 316,000 dead and 1.8 million homeless. The bottom line, of course, was that one of the most impoverished and

historically unfortunate nations in the Americas had suffered a natural calamity of breathtaking proportions. Hundreds of thousands of people remained in "temporary" tent cities 15 months after the event.

If questions still remained about the statistics of Haiti's misery, the deadly quake also posed a more basic question for seismologists: When a natural disaster so devastating hits, oughtn't we have had some way of predicting it? Hurricanes, blizzards, even some volcanic eruptions can be forecast well before their arrival, after all, allowing governments and people to make lifesaving preparations. Earthquakes, however, are stealth disasters, geological phenomena largely undetectable until just seconds before they occur. What scientists have long wanted to know is why quakes are so sneaky and what, if anything, can be done to read any warning signs better.

If any earthquake ought to have been predictable, it was this one. Geologists have been aware of the two clashing tectonic plates that form the Enriquillo–Plantain Garden Fault for decades and have studied them

PORT-AU-PRINCE, 2010 *Two weeks after a big quake devastated Haiti's capital, a man erects a tent in a U.N. refugee camp*

MARCO DORMINO/MINUSTAH VIA GETTY IMAGES

In Japan, a Quake Triggers a Tsunami

SENDAI, JAPAN, 2011 *Shoppers react as a ceiling in a bookstore begins to collapse during the earthquake of March 11*

The undersea earthquake that struck in the Pacific Ocean off the coast of Japan on March 11, 2011, was a monster: it registered 9.0 magnitude, thus becoming the largest quake ever to hit the island nation, topping the famed 1923 quake that claimed 100,000 lives, as well as big quakes in 1948 and 1995. Indeed, it was the fourth largest earthquake since seismologists first started recording their power, around 1900.

Yet it wasn't the earthquake itself that devastated Japan's northeastern regions: it was the giant tsunami waves the quake spawned that swamped the cities along the coast, leaving more than 11,000 dead and 17,000 missing as of late March; the death toll is expected to rise sharply over time. The waves, which reached 30 ft. (9.1 m) in height at some places, either destroyed or severely damaged an estimated 110,000 homes.

The distance that separated the geological event from its consequences is striking: the quake took place some 80 miles (129 km) east of Sendai in the Miyagi prefecture, at a depth of almost 20 miles (32 km) below the ocean floor. Earth scientists were surprised at the quake's location. Japan famously rests upon a tectonic fault line, and big quakes are expect-ed to strike in the Pacific east of Japan, along an undersea area called the Japan Trench, every few decades or so. Indeed, Japan has taken probably the strongest measures of any nation to prepare for earthquakes, enforcing strict building codes and erecting tall seawalls to hold off tsunami waves. But no one expected a 9.0-magnitude quake to strike on the northern end of the trench, and all the authorities' preparations proved inadequate.

After the quake, Shinji Toda, a professor of geology at Kyoto University, told the New York *Times* that a government committee recently concluded that there was a 99 percent chance of a magnitude-7.5 earth-quake in the next 30 years, and warned there was a possibility for an even larger, magnitude-8.0 quake. The 2011 event thus came as a complete surprise. Moreover, according to generally accepted theories, quakes of such a large magnitude are expected to strike along geologically youthful fault lines. Yet the March 2011 quake took place on a fault line that is some 130 million years old, considered quite ancient in geological terms.

Some scientists suspect that the 2011 quake was caused when two tectonic plates in the southern Japan Trench locked together, thus sending the stress—and the eventual quake—farther north. But that is only a theory, and the devastating events that followed the quake and tsunami left many scientists humbled by their inability to predict such disasters. "It's shameful, but we've barely scratched the surface," Ross Stein, a geophysicist with the United States Geological Survey, told the *Times*.

Big Ones
According to the U.S. Geological Survey, these are the five largest earthquakes to strike the planet since 1900

1.	**Chile**	**May 22, 1960**	**9.5** magnitude
2.	**Alaska**	**March 28, 1964**	**9.2** magnitude
3.	**Sumatra**	**Dec. 24, 2006**	**9.1** magnitude
4.	**Japan**	**March 11, 2011**	**9.0** magnitude
5.	**Russia**	**April 11, 1952**	**9.0** magnitude

CHRISTCHURCH, NEW ZEALAND, 2011 *An earthquake on Feb. 22 sent boulders and dirt sliding downhill into a suburban neighborhood*

extensively, and well they should: the fault has shaken the region violently and repeatedly over history. "The plates are shearing the island, grinding it and crushing it," geophysicist Michael Blanpied of the U.S. Geological Survey (USGS) told Time's Jeffrey Kluger. "As that happens, earthquakes pop off."

Monitoring zones like this around the world to get a general sense of where the next such pops may happen is not that difficult, mostly because tectonic activity is hard to conceal completely. There are three types of quakes: the dip-slip fault (in which one clashing plate slides under the other), the reverse dip-slip (in which they pull apart) and the strike-slip (a sideways grinding of the plates). Haiti's quake was a strike-slip, but all three varieties are preceded by years or centuries of accumulated stress, in which the slowly drifting slabs of planet try to shift their position but remain hung up on one another.

The quake occurs when that rock lock is broken. Seismometers can detect the years of stirrings that lead up to that moment, providing some help to geologists.

"We can say things generally about earthquakes," said Blanpied. "We look at faults and patterns of quakes over many years and say where on the landscape they're likeliest to occur next. This forecasting is usually in the long term." Indeed, scientists correctly predicted as recently as 2008 that a fault zone on the south side of Haiti's island of Hispaniola posed a "major seismic hazard."

The problem is, long-term forecasting does not do much to keep people from putting themselves in harm's way. If it did, nobody would live in California or Mexico City or parts of Japan. What's needed is short-term forecasting on the order of weeks, days or hours. And this has stymied scientists again and again.

That failure is reflected in the huge toll big earth-

KOBE, JAPAN, 1995 *An earthquake on Jan. 17, which measured 7.2, killed 6,433 people and twisted elevated railways into ribbons*

EARTHQUAKES 101

IN A "STRIKE-SLIP" fault, right, two plates grinding against each other snap into a new position, sending energy radiating outward in waves. The waves moving inside the earth are **body waves;** when they reach the ground, they are **surface waves.** There are two types of body waves, primary and secondary

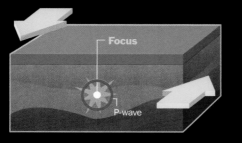

Primary (P) waves travel fast, about 1 to 5 miles per second, arriving first at surface locations. The **focus** is the fracture point belowground; the **epicenter** is the corresponding point aboveground

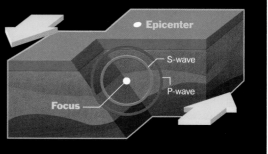

Secondary (S) waves move more slowly, causing the rolling motion of the quake. Surface waves are sometimes called Long waves or L waves; they cause the damage aboveground

quakes can take. On Oct. 8, 2005, a magnitude-7.6 quake struck Kashmir, the politically disputed region in northern Pakistan, killing some 30,000 people in a matter of hours. On Feb. 22, 2011, a 6.3-magnitude temblor struck some 6 miles (10 km) southeast of Christchurch, New Zealand's second-largest city, killing at least 160 people and causing billions of dollars in damage. Three weeks later, on March 11, a 9.0-magnitude quake in the Pacific Ocean triggered a tsunami that devastated Japan's northern coasts, killing more than 11,000 people and leaving an estimated 250,000 homeless.

Like tornadoes, earthquakes are capricious beasts, ruled by what physicists refer to as nonlinear dynamics, which means precise forecasting of when and where they will occur may forever remain impossible. In theory, major earthquakes should be preceded by smaller shocks. They usually are, but the earliest foreshocks are often so weak that they are hard to distinguish from seismic "background noise." And for every small tremor that is followed by a big quake, others are answered by nothing much at all. On an average day, there are more than 50 earthquakes worldwide, almost all of them so slight that they cannot be detected without sensitive instruments.

Even so, geologists are making some headway in their quest to predict big quakes, Blanpied of the USGS told TIME. Instruments that detect P waves are a good example. Earthquakes set off two kinds of seismic vibrations: body waves, which move through the earth's interior, and surface waves, which move on top of the ground. The fastest of the body waves is the P wave, and it's thus the first to travel from the epicenter to a seismic station where it can be detected. P waves don't provide a lot of notice, but even a little can help. In California, gas lines in many homes are now equipped with P-wave detectors, which can sense a coming tremor and shut off the inflow valve to prevent fires and explosions if the house is shaken severely.

For now, the best the USGS and other organizations can do is use the global web of seismometers and other instruments that are already in place (and continue to be improved) to build the best map possible of the planet's interior, and at least narrow the window of when quakes are likely to happen. They can also use these data to anticipate how severe the next tremor, whenever it comes, is likely to be. That can help drive policy decisions like strengthening building codes, reinforcing infrastructure and zoning some areas as unsuitable for development. A narrowing window is hardly the same as precise predicting, but if your home or your life is the one that's spared, it's plenty good enough. ∎

FUKUI, JAPAN, 1948
LIFE *magazine photographer Carl Mydans captured citizens racing for safety as the ground opened during this 7.3-magnitude quake, which left 3,700 dead*

Breaking Ground: Great Earthquakes

SAN FRANCISCO, 1906 Estimated to have peaked at magnitude 7.9, the Great Quake, as city residents still call it, ruptured along a 260-mile (418 km) section of the San Andreas Fault, with the two plates on either side lurching past each other in rifts as wide as 20-ft. (6 m). The deadliest-ever U.S. quake wrecked 29,000 homes, but more destruction was wrought by fire: with the water system offline for more than a week, fire fighters could do little to contain the blazes. Although more than 225,000 people were left homeless, for almost a century the death toll stood at the stunningly low figure of 478. In January 2005, city officials finally acknowledged what historians had long suspected: the low number was made up by civic boosters to downplay the scale of the event. A more accurate death count: 3,000.

YUNGAY, PERU, 1970 It lasted only 45 sec., but that was enough: this earthquake on May 31 was the worst natural disaster in Peruvian history. The epicenter of the quake was in the Pacific Ocean, more than 10 miles (16 km) off the coast, but the 7.9-magnitude event destabilized the northern wall of Mount Huascarán, triggering an avalanche of 80 million cu. yd. of rock, mud and snow. A wall of debris more than 3,000 ft. (914 m) wide and 1 mile long hurtled through Ranrahirca and Yungay at close to 200 m.p.h., completely burying the towns.

In Yungay some villagers were saved by climbing the hill at right, capped with a statue of Christ. More than 70,000 people were killed in the calamity, and an additional 800,000 survivors were left homeless.

MEXICO, 1985 The magnitude-7.8 quake that shook Mexico City on Sept. 19, below, was triggered by a seismic gap, a convergence region that had not experienced a major earthquake for many years but where bottled-up tectonic stress had reached the bursting point. Although the quake's epicenter was on the Pacific Ocean floor about 150 miles (241 km) from Acapulco, coastal towns like Ixtapa suffered much less damage than Mexico City, hundreds of miles inland. Scientists noted that the shoreline is made of solid rock and thus shook less violently, but Mexico's capital city was built on an alluvial lakebed, and as a result, seismic waves were amplified in the city's sediment foundation. Some tall buildings in the huge metropolis vibrated sympathetically with the seismic waves, amplifying their destructive effects. More than 9,000 people died.

CALIFORNIA, 1994 Local mountains rose as much as a foot, nine highways buckled and warped, and 60 people died when a 30-sec. earthquake rocked Northridge, a suburb of Los Angeles. Multistory buildings like the one above simply pancaked. Some 3.1 million people were left in darkness, and an oil main and 250 gas lines ruptured. More than 1,000 aftershocks, some considerable temblors in their own right, kept the ground shaking long after the main event. Yet California is perched atop such a perilous convergence zone that this quake was far from "the Big One" that disturbs the dreams of Golden Staters.

FROM TOP: LES STONE—CORBIS SYGMA; DAVID WOO—DALLAS MORNING NEWS/CORBIS; RONG SHOUJUN—XINHUA—GAMMA

PAKISTAN, 2005 After a 7.6 quake rattled Kashmir on Oct. 8, citizens searched for survivors in the ruins of a collapsed 10-story building in Islamabad, right. By the onset of winter, more than 87,000 people were dead and some 3 million were homeless. Relief efforts were set back by the region's remoteness, tribal infighting, local corruption and a tepid response by the international community. "We thought the [2004 Indian Ocean] tsunami was bad," said U.N. aid coordinator Jan Egeland. "This is worse."

Portals of Fire

Gateways to a molten world, volcanoes bring forth
fresh land from within the planet, often at a cost

T HERE IS NO MORE CONVINCING—AND NO
more devastating—evidence that we inhabit a
living planet than the restless, unpredictable
and occasionally cataclysmic activity of volcanoes. Everywhere around the globe, including under the
oceans, the planet's crust is constantly breaking open,
spewing forth the raw material of new plains, plateaus,
seabeds and mountains, then subsiding into itself, or
rumbling furtively, in sounds that can augur imminent
destruction or may mean nothing at all. Small wonder,
volcanoes are enduring symbols of nature's raw power.
Mountains of fire erupt time and again in humanity's
legends and stories: the god Vulcan of Roman mythology
lent his name to them, and volcanoes play central roles in

MESSINA, SICILY *Italy's Mount Etna, one of the most active volcanoes on the globe, erupts over the populous area*

the Norse sagas, the German *Nibelungenlied,* the operas of Richard Wagner and in such recent incarnations as Mount Doom in J.R.R. Tolkien's *Lord of the Rings* trilogy.

More than 1,500 active volcanoes dot our planet's landmasses, hundreds more lie beneath its seas, and an unknown number of others are lying dormant or gestating deep within the earth, waiting to be born. On average, a volcano erupts somewhere in the world once each week. Most gently spill lava—molten rock—down their slopes; some explode with a force many times greater than all the world's nuclear weapons combined.

One goal of the scientists who study volcanoes is to predict when one of them will blow its top, and with how much force it will do so. Unfortunately, there is no substitute for close examination, and what little volcanologists have learned over the centuries has often come at a fearsome price. Beginning in A.D. 79, when the Roman naturalist Pliny the Elder was killed while observing an eruption of Mount Vesuvius, volcanology has been one of the world's more dangerous fields of study. In an average year, at least one volcano scientist is killed in the field.

Yet despite the danger volcanoes pose, humans have been drawn to them since ancient times. The surrounding soils are mineral rich, and dried volcanic mud and lava flows often form flat areas, conducive to settlement. Today about 500 million people (1 of every 14 of the planet's population) live close enough to an active volcano to be in danger. The two volcanoes with today's deadliest potential are both active and perilously close to large population centers: Italy's Mount Vesuvius towers over Naples and its surrounding towns, home to more than 11 million people, while Africa's Nyiragongo volcano glowers over the Congolese city of Goma. But these two are hardly unique: Mexico City sits in the shadow of Popocatépetl, which has been growling for years and could someday rain ash and rock on the homes of 20 million people. But few volcanoes can be safely ignored. Among the world's known active cones, more than one-third have erupted violently in the past 400 years.

Most volcanoes, like earthquakes, occur where the planet's tectonic plates grind against one another. Thus they are especially common in the same areas where quakes are prevalent, such as the Pacific Ocean's Ring of

HOT STUFF *At left, lava from Hawaii's Kilauea, which erupts almost constantly, flows into the sea; at right, molten lava*

An Eruption in Iceland Shuts Down the Skies

As modern civilization becomes ever more inter-connected, natural events that once might have passed without notice can spark major global headaches. That message was driven home early in 2010, when the relatively routine eruption of a volcano in Iceland led to a worldwide travel crisis.

The rumbles from the island nation's Eyjafjallajokull volcano began late in 2009, but it wasn't until April 14 of 2010 that its cone began percolating with significant power, spewing gigantic columns of ash into the sky. The ash cloud put on quite a show, but as volcanoes go, the eruption of the 5,466-ft. (1,666 m) Eyjafjallajokull, or Eyja, for short, won't make the history books. Scientists measured it at 2 or 3 on the Volcanic Explosivity Index, which ranks volcanic events on a 1-to-8 scale. Eyja's blast barely compared with major eruptions like Mount St. Helens in 1980, which killed 57 people and devastated hundreds of square miles of forest, or the catastrophe of Krakatoa in Indonesia in 1883, which killed more than 40,000 people and was felt around the world when suspended ash in the stratosphere actually lowered global temper-atures for more than a year.

In contrast, Eyja's eruption caused no deaths, and just 800 people living near the volcano, along with horses owned by local ranchers, had to be evacuated. Even so the medium-sized eruption on tiny Iceland—an island formed by ancient eruptions that sits atop one of the planet's largest tectonic rifts—had an enormous impact on the world. As its 7-mile (11.3 km) -high plume of volcanic gases and silicate ash spread across much of Europe, it brought air travel across the Continent to a near standstill for a week, as authorities grounded planes. (Even relatively small amounts of volcanic ash high in the air can clog sensitive jet engines, disabling ventilation and causing the machinery to melt down and fail.)

Eurocontrol, the aviation body that coordinates flights in Europe, estimates that 6,000 of the 28,000 daily flights across Europe were canceled on Thursday, April 15. In Britain, authorities forbade all nonemergency flights to and from the country. At London's Heathrow Airport, one of the world's busiest, the eruption affected 1,200 flights and some 180,000 passengers. Civil-aviation authorities in Belgium, Denmark, France, Germany, Ireland, Finland, Norway and Sweden closed all or parts of their airspaces. The chaos affected trav-elers in the Asia-Pacific region too, as flights to Europe were canceled. The problems were estimated to have cost the global air-travel industry $200 million a day. Not bad for a minor-league eruption.

The havoc caused by Eyja is a reminder that in our increasingly networked world, it's less the sheer power of a natural disaster than where and when it happens—and how prepared we are to respond—that matter. If the volcano had erupted in the years before air travel became common, it wouldn't have been noticed outside Iceland.

Fire. They are most often found where huge slabs of the earth's crust are subducted, or forced downward, into the planet's superheated interior, where they melt. Because this molten rock, or magma, is lighter than the material that surrounds it, it is buoyant and rises back toward the surface. There it can sit, undetected, for millions of years. But when accumulating pressure underground becomes too great, the liquefied rock finds a weak spot in the earth's surface, which buckles upward and eventually explodes as a volcano. Not all volcanoes trace the planet's

fault lines, however; some sit atop "hot spots" where stable reservoirs of magma lie close to the earth's surface. The Hawaiian archipelago was formed by such volcanoes.

Although the science of predicting eruptions is young, progress has been made by focusing on the small earthquakes that precede most eruptions. Using seismographs, acoustic sensors, and GPS navigation beacons, volcanologists have learned to recognize a signature of distinctive tremors that almost always precede a violent eruption. The signals come in two forms: A-type, which begins with a sharp crack and then trails off quickly; and B-type, which builds slowly and then trails off gradually.

These signals, scientists believe, correspond, respectively, to the crumbling of solid rock under the upward pressure exerted by liquefied rock and the liquefied rock slowly filling the cracks made by the crumbling action. A repeating pattern of A-type and B-type readings, coming one after another with increasing rapidity, like the contractions of a woman going into labor, helped scientists anticipate the 2000 eruption of Mexico's Popocatépetl. Interpreting the signals given off by the volcano since 1993, scientists were able to peg the exact date of the Dec. 18 eruption two days in advance.

MOUNT DOOM *At top, volcanologists pose for a snapshot before descending into the cone of Colombia's Galeras volcano in 1993, which erupted during their journey. Standing, from left: Alfredo Manzo, Nestor Garcia, Fabio Garcia, Igor Menyailov; seated, Stanley Williams and José Arles Zapata. Not shown: Andrew McFarlane. Below, Galeras smokes in 2005*

FIRE AND WATER *Hawaii's Kilauea is a very active but relatively tame volcano, providing tourists with a spectacular clash of elements*

The early warning provided enough time for the Mexican army to evacuate more than 30,000 people from the most threatened areas. Just as important, scientists were able to estimate the severity of the event, accurately predicting it would be a moderate eruption. Thus no needless evacuations were ordered.

Yet some eruptions occur with little notice, and one such event in January 1993 ended in tragedy. The site was the 13,680-ft. (4.1 km) Galeras volcano in the Colombian Andes, which had experienced a few minor eruptions in the previous six months. Before that, aside from a significant blow in 1988, Galeras had been almost completely dormant for more than 40 years.

So when a team of 13 scientists attending a nearby United Nations conference on volcano prediction set out to descend into the volcano's cone to collect data, they believed they were not placing themselves in significant danger. They even allowed a group of tourists to join them as they climbed down into the cone. The expedition was led by Arizona State University geologist Stanley Williams and included Florida International University earth scientist Andrew McFarlane, as well as Igor Menyailov, a Russian expert from the Institute of Volcanology in Petropav-

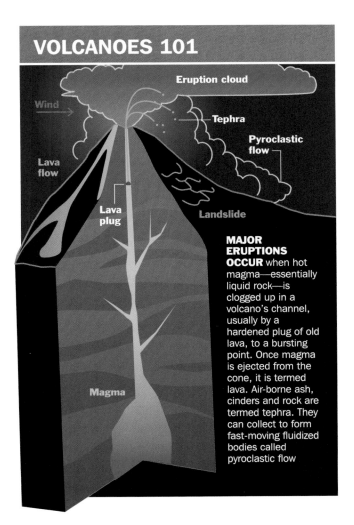

VOLCANOES 101

Eruption cloud

Wind

Tephra

Pyroclastic flow

Lava flow

Lava plug

Landslide

Magma

MAJOR ERUPTIONS OCCUR when hot magma—essentially liquid rock—is clogged up in a volcano's channel, usually by a hardened plug of old lava, to a bursting point. Once magma is ejected from the cone, it is termed lava. Air-borne ash, cinders and rock are termed tephra. They can collect to form fast-moving fluidized bodies called pyroclastic flow

THE RING OF FIRE

Tracing the seams where giant tectonic plates collide, a crescent of volcanoes encircles the Pacific

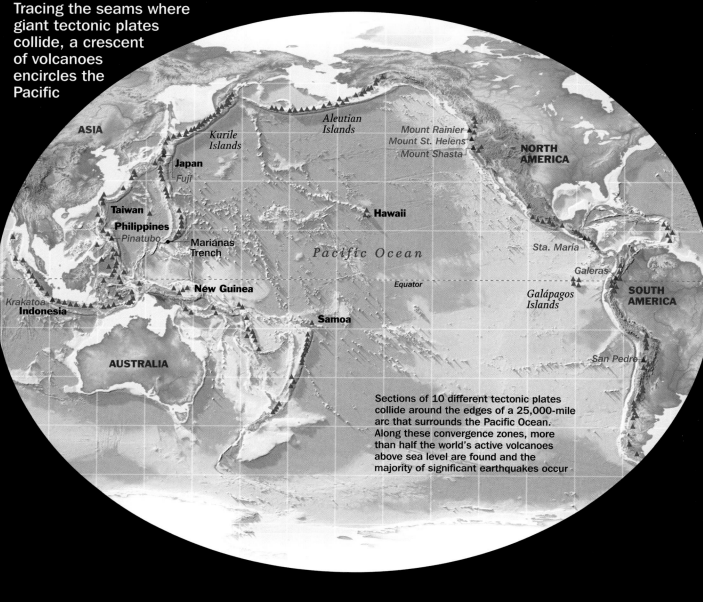

ASIA

Kurile Islands

Aleutian Islands

Mount Rainier
Mount St. Helens
Mount Shasta

NORTH AMERICA

Japan
Fuji

Taiwan

Philippines
Pinatubo

Marianas Trench

Hawaii

Pacific Ocean

Sta. María

Galeras

New Guinea

Equator

Galápagos Islands

SOUTH AMERICA

Krakatoa
Indonesia

Samoa

AUSTRALIA

San Pedro

Sections of 10 different tectonic plates collide around the edges of a 25,000-mile arc that surrounds the Pacific Ocean. Along these convergence zones, more than half the world's active volcanoes above sea level are found and the majority of significant earthquakes occur

---

lovsk on the geologically active Kamchatka Peninsula.

Shortly after 1 p.m., having spent about four hours inside the volcano's cone, the scientists were relaxing when suddenly a single rock tumbled from the rim above them and landed inside the crater. It was followed by another, then another. In the next few seconds, jets of searing gas blew straight up from beneath their feet, as tons of stone were blasted skyward. "Suddenly there were these big rocks, the size of television sets and baseballs, flying through the air at hundreds of miles an hour," Williams recalled for TIME years later. "And they were on fire." Within a few seconds, Menyailov was incinerated, along with Colombian scientist Nestor Garcia; both of their re-

mains vaporized into gas. A local college professor, Carlos Trujillo, was cut in half by falling debris.

In all, six scientists who trekked inside the cone of Galeras that morning died, along with three members of the tourist party. Both McFarlane and Williams survived—in the latter's case, just barely. "I was marginally alive," recalled Williams, who was covered with burns. When rescuers finally reached the scene, they found Williams' backpack, altimeter and sunglasses melted onto his body.

When the survivors reached Pasto, the town that lies at the foot of the volcano, they were told that the inferno they had experienced was a minor eruption; nothing special. Galeras, it seems, had barely shrugged. ■

Blastoff: Great Eruptions

POMPEII, ITALY Italy's Mount Vesuvius exploded in A.D. 79, burying the cities of Pompeii and Herculaneum and preserving citizens in the very postures in which they were buried in ash. The preserved ruins of the towns offer an enduring window into life in the Roman Empire at its height—while Vesuvius continues to rumble, and remains one of the world's most threatening active volcanoes.

KRAKATOA, INDONESIA In the most powerful modern eruption, this volcano in the Sunda Strait exploded beginning on Aug. 27, 1883. The force of the blast altered the shape of the archipelago, sent deadly tsunamis across the region and spewed so much ash into the air that the sun was dimmed and temperatures around the globe were reduced for more than a year.

PINATUBO, THE PHILIPPINES The volcano on the island of Luzon erupted with massive power in 1991, killing as many as 300 people, injuring hundreds more and displacing millions. Before the eruption, the volcano was inconspicuous and was not considered to pose a threat. It was the second largest eruption of the 20th century; the largest was the 1912 eruption of Novarupta in Alaska.

Blast From The Past

A supervolcano may make
Yellowstone rock and roll again

WE'RE STILL FINDING BURIED ASH deposits more than 20 ft. deep in California and all over the Great Plains," Bob Christiansen said of a volcano that exploded in what is now Yellowstone National Park 640,000 years ago. "It covered most of the western United States in a blanket of hot ash," Christiansen, a scientist emeritus at the U.S. Geological Survey, told TIME in 2006, "and even did significant damage east the Mississippi," where scientists have uncovered shallower layers of rock and ash in Louisiana and Mississippi. "For comparison," he noted, "when Mount St. Helens erupted in 1980, it threw 1 cu km (0.386 sq. mi.) of rock and ash into the air." The

Yellowstone supervolcano, as such massive eruptions are called, "tossed around 2,000 cu km (772 sq. mi.) of debris and ejecta into the atmosphere," Christiansen said. "So we're talking about a level of force that is several thousand times greater than any volcano that has erupted during recorded human history."

In technical terms, a supervolcano is a volcano that erupts with magnitude 8 or greater on the Volcanic Explosivity Index, which means that more than 1,000 cu km (386 sq. mi.) of lava and ash are blown out of the cone. The Yellowstone eruption left a hole in the ground more than 35 miles (56 km) wide. This structure, known as the Yellowstone caldera, is so large that it went unnoticed until the 1960s, when it was first detected in satellite photo-

JEFF VANUGA—CORBIS

52

rock." Such enormous blasts obviously wreak havoc in the region surrounding the event, but they can also alter the climate of the entire globe.

"There's a lot of evidence that the eruption of Krakatoa in 1883, which was not a supervolcano, changed the climate of the entire world for several years," Christiansen said. "The ash in the upper atmosphere is highly reflective, which means that less sunlight reaches the surface of the earth, until the ash has fallen back to the surface. And this can take several years." Written records note such "little Ice Ages," lasting from one to four years, not only in the wake of Krakatoa but also following eruptions in Iceland in 1783 and Indonesia in 1815.

"If you scale the same effects up to account for the increased power of a supervolcano," Christiansen pointed out, "you're talking about catastrophic effects on the climate around the world, lasting for decades, maybe centuries." Indeed, Stanley Ambrose, an anthropologist at the University of Illinois at Urbana-Champaign, has theorized that after the Toba supervolcano erupted, the worldwide population of *Homo sapiens* dwindled to just a few thousand and modern man nearly became extinct. In Ambrose's view, that explains why all human beings appear to be genetically related to a relatively small number of common ancestors.

After the eruption of a supervolcano, the underground chamber that housed its several thousand cu km of liquefied rock usually collapses, leaving a vast depression in the planet's surface, like the Yellowstone caldera. Such depressions can be found in more than a dozen places around the globe, most of them above the hot spots where mantle plumes (pools of molten rock welling up from deep beneath the planet's crust) rise toward the surface.

The bad news: a team of U.S. geologists warned in 2001 that the Yellowstone caldera remains active and is likely to erupt at some point in the future. Such a blast would cover up to half of the U.S. in a layer of rock and ash at least 3 ft. (0.9 m) deep, although they declined to predict when it will occur. The good news: it doesn't appear to be anytime soon. "These are extremely rare events," said Christiansen. "And all the evidence we now have says that the event would be preceded by decades, if not centuries, of warning signs. So it's true that a supervolcano will again erupt somewhere in the world someday. But it's not something we have to worry about in the foreseeable future." Feel free to exhale. ∎

graphs. "Supervolcanoes usually don't take the shape of mountains, the way ordinary volcanoes do," Christiansen explained. "They are caused by the uplift of massive pools of molten rock, rising from deep within the earth. Often they appear to take the form of the ground bulging over a large area, until it simply explodes."

And when that happens, as has twice occurred in Yellowstone—the earlier blast was about 2 million years ago—"every living thing within a radius of hundreds of miles dies almost immediately," Christiansen said. "For thousands of miles around, environments are radically transformed. The eruption of the Toba supervolcano [in Sumatra, around 74,000 years ago, the most recent such event] covered most of Southeast Asia with ash and

Perhaps because man is a creature of the land, we see our globe as a group of seven large continents separated by oceans and seas. Yet that's a flawed perspective, for Earth is a water planet on which the continents are the minority partner. There is a vantage point in space, high above the South Pacific Ocean, from which astronauts can regard the planet whole and see it in proper balance—as a brilliant indigo sphere of water fringed by a ring of land, Asia and Australia to the left, the Americas to the right. On this blue world, life depends on water: just as it accounts for 70% of the surface of the planet, water makes up more than half the human body. That reliance makes us subject to the delicate operations of climate and geography that keep us wet: rivers and lakes, springs and aquifers, monsoon rains and ocean currents.

THE WATER PLANET

MISSISSIPPI RIVER DELTA, 2001 *This picture, taken by a camera that records heat emissions, shows the river as a broad diagonal strip. The green areas are mud and marshland*

Drought Stalks the Rain Forest

AMAZON RIVER BASIN, BRAZIL In the first decade of the 21st century, areas along the Amazon River suffered from the worst drought in the area's recorded history, leaving boats stranded on high ground, horses parched and tributaries dry. These pictures were taken in October 2005 near the confluence of the Amazon and Madeira rivers, seen at top right. Scientists could not identify a single direct cause of the drought, but prominent suspects included the buildup of warm waters in tropical seas, the deforestation of South America's rain forests and the gradual warming of the globe.

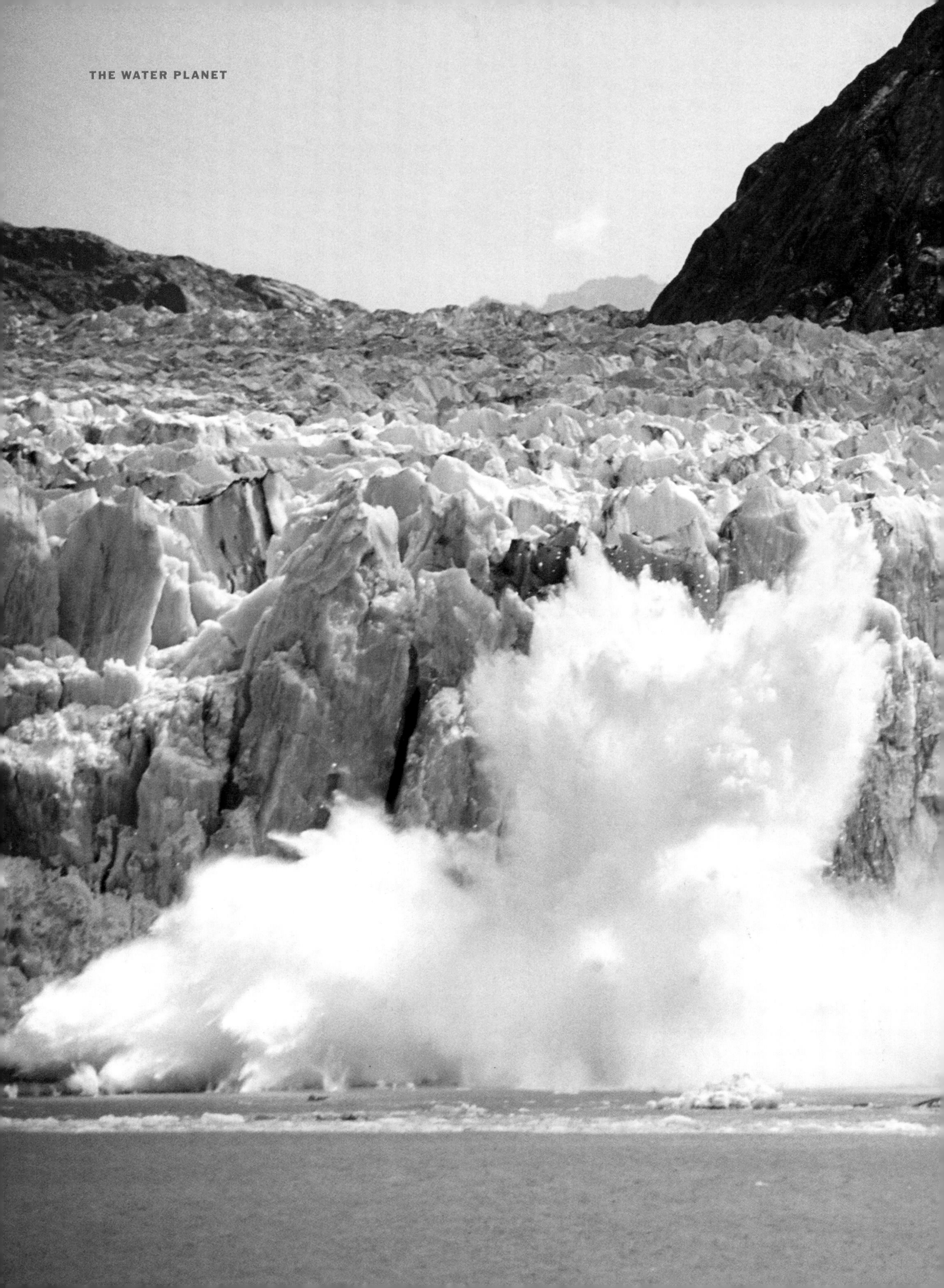

A Glacier Runs Through It

SOUTH SAWYER GLACIER, ALASKA Glaciers are rivers of ice; this one flows, slowly, into the waters of the Stephens Passage south of Juneau. Tidewater glaciers like South Sawyer can move as fast as 7 ft. (2.1 m) a day, constantly calving and sending icebergs up to 200 ft. (61 m) high thundering into the bay. When explorer George Vancouver visited it in 1794, today's open bay was frozen, choked with glaciers; by 1879 naturalist John Muir found that the ice had moved 48 miles (77 km) up the bay. The retreat continues.

CARL & ANN PURCELL–CORBIS

Swept Away

COLUMBIA, ILLINOIS, 1993 The great flood along the Mississippi River in 1927 was one of the most devastating natural disasters in U.S. history. The "Old Man" overflowed its banks again, in 1993, in a "500-year flood" after as much as 10 times the normal rainfall fell over eight Midwestern states in about two months. More than 10 million acres of land were immersed; hundreds of federal and private levees burst—and raging waters uprooted the farmhouse shown at left from its foundations, sheared it in half and bore it away.

Waters Of Woe

Humanity's works are no match for the power of tsunami waves

KOJI HAGA WASN'T JUST CLOSE TO THE tsunami that devastated northern Japan on March 11, 2011. He was on top of it. Somehow the fishing-boat captain kept his pitching vessel upright as the churning force of the wave attacked the shore, turning his coastal community of Akaushi into a graveyard of rubble and leaving some 27,000 people dead or missing in the country's northern prefectures. TIME's Hannah Beech met Haga barely 24 hours after he'd returned to the spot where his house once stood. Aside from the roof, which landed not far from Haga's building's foundations, Beech reported, there was nothing recognizable that remained of his home. A few mementos were scattered in the kaleidoscopic wreckage: his waterlogged family albums were lodged in the axle of an upturned car, while his daughter's pink stuffed animal lay facedown in the mud.

As Beech watched, Haga ignored most of these keepsakes. His first priority was scooping up sodden rice to take back to his hungry family and neighbors, who had escaped the wave by scrambling to higher ground. Yet even as the fisherman packed the ruined grain into a sack, he displayed the fortitude and generosity that distinguished this devastated region of Japan in the wake of the tsunami: Haga was embarrassed that the rice was spoiled, but he invited Beech to take some. The next day, Haga would join Akaushi's other survivors to begin the slow clearing of debris and then the reconstruction of a village virtually wiped off the map. "We'll all try our best to do this together," he said, not a note of pity in his voice. "That's the Japanese way, isn't it?"

Haga and his fellow Japanese were living through the

THE SURGE *The tsunami crashes ashore in Iwanuma in Miyagi prefecture. The waves speed up as they near the shore*

KYODO—REUTERS—LANDOV

NATORI, JAPAN *A woman grieves amid the devastation created by the tsunami. Opposite page: scenes from the aftermath*

gravest natural disaster in their nation's history, a three-headed monster consisting of a huge undersea earthquake, a massive tsunami and a nuclear crisis. The nation's ordeal began at 2:46 p.m. on March 11, when a magnitude-9.0 quake—the largest in Japan's recorded history and the planet's fourth-largest quake since 1900, occurred in the Japan Trench, a subduction zone off the east coast of the Japanese archipelago.

As seismologist Alice Walker at the British Geological Survey in Edinburgh explained to TIME, a subduction zone is where one tectonic plate is moving under another, and the March 11 event was a 'thrust' earthquake, a variety of a "dip-slip" quake, in which the ground is actually thrust upward, causing surface deformation of the seabed. The displacement at the surface caused by this deformation excites a big column of water—a tsunami.

These killer waves are stealthy: they can travel hundreds or even thousands of miles across the ocean at speeds of up to 500 m.p.h., almost undetectable as long as they remain submerged in the deep, for they are essentially widespread, massive increases in the volume of water, rather than the curling waves we are used to see breaking upon shorelines. But when the massive swells approach the uphill slopes that link shorelines to the ocean floor, tsunamis compress and speed up, racing up the incline and emerging from the surf as giant walls of water bearing overwhelming power, forces of mass plus energy that can destroy everything in their path.

And that's what happened on March 11 across the coastlines of northeastern Japan. The temblor, centered 20 miles (32 km) below the surface, caused a 23-ft. (7 m) tsunami that swept through coastal areas in Fukushima prefecture, and a 13-ft. (3.9 m) tsunami in nearby Iwate prefecture. Dramatic aerial images over Miyagi prefecture, which is largely flat farmland, showed a dark, debris-filled sea of water and mud enveloping everything in its path, from houses to schools, cars and roads. Seldom has nature's dominion over the works of human beings been more apparent, more widely and closely documented on video—or more heartbreaking.

In the weeks that followed, an anxious world watched Japan struggle to dig out from its natural tragedy even as it fought a tragedy abetted by human technology, as workers strained to control damaged reactors at the nuclear power plant in Fukushima. By month's end, the toll

from the earthquake and tsunami stood at more than 11,000 dead and 16,000 missing, and few doubted that the number of missing would decrease as the number of confirmed dead rose. More than 2,000 bodies had been recovered from the sea, authorities reported, and some 240,000 people were homeless, sheltered in about 1,900 evacuation centers spread mainly across the battered northeast but also in cities like Tokyo. The government estimated the damage at $300 billion, which would make it the most expensive natural disaster on record.

Perched on the Ring of Fire, an arc of seismic activity that encircles the Pacific Basin, Japan is one of the most earthquake-prone countries in the world, and it has long been regarded as one of the best equipped to handle whatever is thrown at it. Having survived the great Tokyo quake of 1923, which killed at least 100,000 people; the utter devastation of World War II; and, in 1995, an earthquake in Kobe that took more than 6,400 lives, Japan has been a world leader in disaster preparedness.

Every year since 1960, Japan has observed Disaster Prevention Day on Sept. 1, the anniversary of the 1923 quake. The nation also boasts the world's most sophisticated earthquake early-warning systems, and it has consistently upgraded its building codes to spare lives during earthquakes. During the March 11 quake the skyscrapers of Tokyo, about 231 miles (373 km) from the epicenter, were badly rattled, swaying to and fro. But the buildings stood, a tribute to the nation's preparedness.

Japan also boasts a tsunami warning service, set up in 1952, that consists of 300 sensors around the archipelago, including 80 aquatic sensors that monitor seismic activity 24/7. The network is designed to predict the height, speed, location and arrival time of any tsunami heading for the nation's coast. On Japan's east coast, where tsunamis frequently hit, hundreds of earthquake and tsunami-proof shelters have been built. Some cities have built tsunami walls and floodgates, so that the waves don't travel inland through river systems. But as videos showed in horrifying detail, the seawalls and floodgates weren't built to withstand the power of a tsunami as mighty as the March 11 monster, which simply overwhelmed them.

The 2011 Tsunami Triggers a Nuclear Crisis

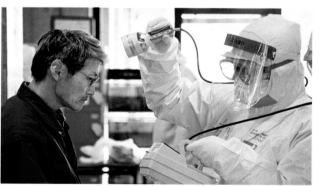

THE TSUNAMI THAT struck northern Japan on March 11, 2011, not only devastated coastal towns but also spawned a nuclear crisis, as waves crashed into six reactors at the Fukushima Daiichi nuclear power plant, above, shutting down power lines that fed systems that cooled the reactors. The breakdown spawned grave fears of a nuclear meltdown and possible release of radioactive matter. As this book went to press in early April, no meltdown had occurred, but there was no question that radioactive matter was leaking from the plant, workers were still struggling to cool down the reactors, and the outcome was far from certain. As concern mounted that at least one containment vessel for fuel rods may have

been breached, authorities extended the evacuation zone around the plant, established early in the crisis, from 12 to 18 miles (20 to 30 km).

In Japan, unsafe radiation levels were found in tap water as far away as Tokyo, 136 miles (219 km) south of the Fukushima plant; above, a man is screened for radiation levels in Koriyama City in Fukushima prefecture. Milk and leafy vegetables from Fukushima had been banned both nationally and abroad. In late March, Yukiya Amano, director-general of the Geneva-based International Atomic Energy Agency, told the New York *Times:* "This is a very serious accident by all standards, and it is not over yet."

LANDFALL *The tsunami, sweeping all before it, breaches an embankment in Miyako in Iwate prefecture on March 11*

Tsunami is a Japanese word meaning "great harbor wave." Because tsunamis resemble the rising level of water associated with incoming tides, they are often referred to as "tidal waves," but the term is a misnomer. However imperfectly understood, tsunamis have shaped human history. Giant waves spawned by earthquakes are believed by some scholars to have submerged ancient cities in the Mediterranean, which may have given rise to the legend of Atlantis. On All Saints' Day in 1775, the great earthquake that flattened the city of Lisbon triggered a tsunami that flooded much of coastal Spain and Portugal. But earthquakes are not the only cause of killer waves: the eruption of the Krakatoa volcano in 1883 stirred up a tsunami that drowned 36,000 people and hurled 600-ton blocks of coral ashore as if they were pebbles.

More recently, on Dec. 26, 2004, the deadliest disaster of the 21st century took place in nations surrounding the Indian Ocean. As with the 2011 tsunami in Japan, the events began with an earthquake some 18 miles (29 km) beneath the surface of the ocean, where two vast pieces of the earth's crust—the Indian Plate and the Burma

Plate—converge. The Indian Plate, which usually moves northeast about 2.4 in. (6 cm) a year, twice the rate at which our fingernails grow, had instead lurched more than 50 ft. (15 m) in the course of a few seconds. That had forced the Burma Plate to snap upward along 745 miles (1,199 km) of the fault line, setting off an earthquake that eventually measured 9.1 on the Richter scale and triggered 68 aftershocks within three days. The killer waves unleashed by the undersea earthquake inundated shorelines in a great circular swath around the Indian Ocean, and when they finally receded, more than 225,000 people were dead.

Can we learn to predict such killer waves? Serious scientific attempts to do so date back to the April Fools' Day tsunami of 1946. That day a medium-strength earthquake off the coast of Alaska's Aleutian Islands sent powerful waves racing across the Pacific. One crashed into the Aleutians at a height of 139 ft. (42 m) but did little damage in the sparsely inhabited area. The Hawaiian Islands weren't so lucky. When one of the waves reached the Big Island, five hours after the quake, it reared up to a height of 45 ft. (13.7 m) and tore through the coastal communities of Hilo and Haena, killing 159 people.

The deadly event led to the creation of the Seismic Sea Wave Warning System, which later became known as the Pacific Tsunami Warning Center (PTWC). For 65 years, PTWC scientists have been struggling not only to predict future tsunamis but also to understand the 1946 event. Their question: How could a moderate earthquake spawn such a powerful wave? For decades, the best theory was that the quake had triggered an undersea landslide, and that one-two punch had driven the tsunami. But in 2004, an undersea expedition mounted by the Scripps Institution of Oceanography visited the quake site and found no evidence of a landslide. So PTWC scientists are going back to Square One as they seek to explain the 1946 wave.

In recent years scientists have begun to link the threat of tsunamis to global climate change, pointing to seabed landslides as the link between the two. Archaeological evidence indicates that "megatsunamis," killer waves more than 1,000 ft. (305 m) high, emerged from the oceans in ancient times. The best guess about what may have caused them is massive undersea landslides. The most recent megatsunamis may have been unleashed around 6100 B.C., when the Storegga Slides, a series of sudden undersea land shifts off the coast of what is now Norway, appear to have sent massive waves rushing across the North Atlantic. Because warmer air and water temperatures are associated with landslides, both undersea and on land, there is a chance that future climate change could trigger a tsunami the likes of which our world has not experienced in recorded history.

In the meantime, the struggle to understand the tsunamis we have experienced goes on. Less than 90 days after the 2004 Indian Ocean quake and tsunami, a stronger earthquake shook the same area, its epicenter just 60 miles (96 km) south of the earlier one. That led the PTWC to issue an urgent bulletin, and within hours tens of thousands of people had heeded orders to abandon their homes for higher ground. Yet while the temblor shook the ground from Indonesia to Thailand, it was not followed by a major tsunami. One theory as to the discrepancy: an earthquake's wavelength—the frequency at which it shakes the ground—may have more effect on a subsequent tsunami than the quake's magnitude. But that is far from certain. What is certain is that we still have much to learn about the waves that can suddenly emerge from the deep and erase thousands of human lives. ∎

PHUKET, THAILAND *Resort waiter Supet Gatemanee, 19, battles giant waves on Dec. 26, 2004; he survived the ordeal*

2004: HOW THE DEADLY WAVES SPREAD

SCOPE OF THE TRAGEDY

As of 2011, the U.S. Geological Survey estimated the number of dead in the 2004 tsunami at 227,898. Indonesia was the nation hardest-hit in the disaster

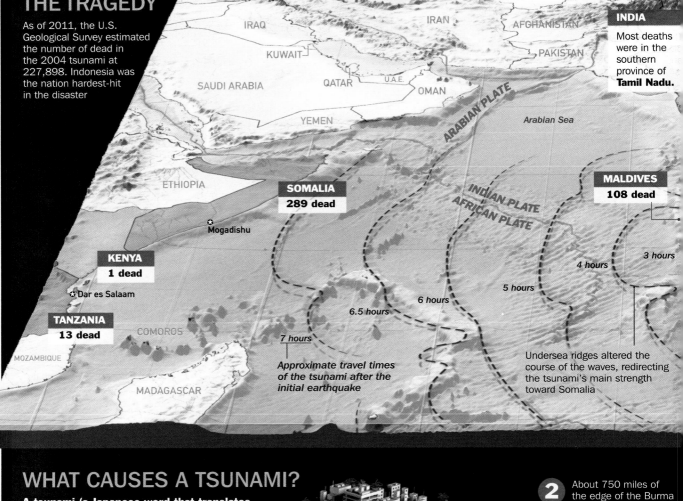

IRAQ

IRAN

AFGHANISTAN

INDIA

Most deaths were in the southern province of **Tamil Nadu.**

KUWAIT

PAKISTAN

QATAR

U.A.E.

SAUDI ARABIA

OMAN

YEMEN

Arabian Sea

ARABIAN PLATE

ETHIOPIA

SOMALIA
289 dead

INDIAN PLATE
AFRICAN PLATE

MALDIVES
108 dead

✪ Mogadishu

3 hours

4 hours

KENYA
1 dead

5 hours

⊛ Dar es Salaam

6 hours

TANZANIA
13 dead

6.5 hours

COMOROS

MOZAMBIQUE

7 hours

MADAGASCAR

Approximate travel times of the tsunami after the initial earthquake

Undersea ridges altered the course of the waves, redirecting the tsunami's main strength toward Somalia

WHAT CAUSES A TSUNAMI?

A tsunami (a Japanese word that translates as "harbor wave") is triggered by a vertical disturbance in the ocean, such as an earthquake, landslide or volcanic eruption

2 About 750 miles of the edge of the Burma Plate snapped, forcing **a massive displacement of water** in the Indian Ocean

BURMA PLATE

Stress builds as one plate pulls down on the other

INDIAN PLATE

 1 The disaster was caused by a massive **earthquake** off the coast of Indonesia, where two **plates** of the earth's crust grind against each other

Sources: Vasily Titov, National Oceanic and Atmospheric Administration; U.S. Geological Survey; AP; Reuters; Globalsecurity.org; University of Washington

TIME Graphic by Joe Lertola, Ed Gabel and Jackson Dykman

The most powerful earthquake in 40 years quickly turned into one of the worst disasters in a century, as walls of water crashed ashore across South Asia

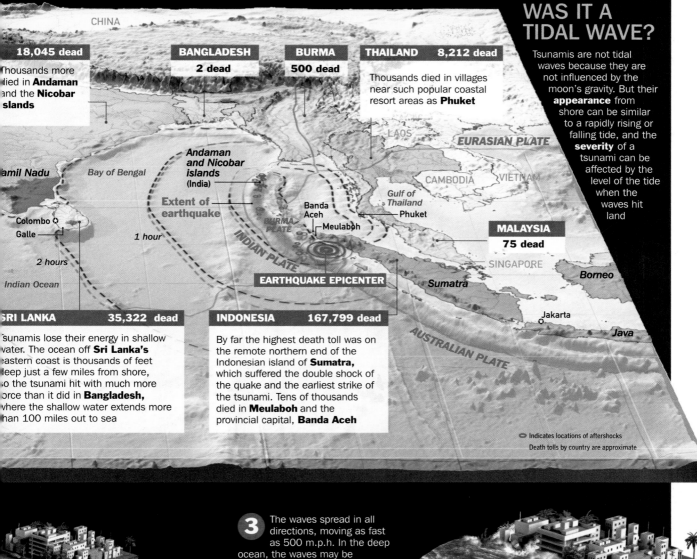

WAS IT A TIDAL WAVE?

Tsunamis are not tidal waves because they are not influenced by the moon's gravity. But their **appearance** from shore can be similar to a rapidly rising or falling tide, and the **severity** of a tsunami can be affected by the level of the tide when the waves hit land

CHINA

18,045 dead
Thousands more died in **Andaman** and the **Nicobar islands**

BANGLADESH
2 dead

BURMA
500 dead

THAILAND   **8,212 dead**
Thousands died in villages near such popular coastal resort areas as **Phuket**

Tamil Nadu

Bay of Bengal

Andaman and Nicobar islands (India)

Extent of earthquake

LAOS

EURASIAN PLATE

CAMBODIA   VIETNAM

Gulf of Thailand

Colombo

Galle

1 hour

Banda Aceh
Meulaboh

Phuket

BURMA PLATE

INDIAN PLATE

2 hours

Indian Ocean

EARTHQUAKE EPICENTER

Sumatra

MALAYSIA
75 dead

SINGAPORE

Borneo

Jakarta

Java

AUSTRALIAN PLATE

SRI LANKA   **35,322 dead**
Tsunamis lose their energy in shallow water. The ocean off **Sri Lanka's** eastern coast is thousands of feet deep just a few miles from shore, so the tsunami hit with much more force than it did in **Bangladesh,** where the shallow water extends more than 100 miles out to sea

INDONESIA   **167,799 dead**
By far the highest death toll was on the remote northern end of the Indonesian island of **Sumatra,** which suffered the double shock of the quake and the earliest strike of the tsunami. Tens of thousands died in **Meulaboh** and the provincial capital, **Banda Aceh**

◯ Indicates locations of aftershocks
Death tolls by country are approximate

3 The waves spread in all directions, moving as fast as 500 m.p.h. In the deep ocean, the waves may be imperceptible, but they slow down and gain height as they hit **shallow water** near shore

Sudden movement forces water up and down

The retreat of a tsunami from land can be quick— and just as dangerous as its approach. The waves often come in a series

In deep water tsunamis are very long, shallow waves, which means they don't lose much energy fighting gravity. Given enough initial force, they will travel vast distances until they are slowed by resistance from the sea floor near shore

A GIANT JOLT

The Indian plate usually moves northeast about 2.4 in. a year. Scientists estimate that in last week's quake, the two plates slid about 50 ft. at once

Drawings are not to scale

The Next Wave: Megatsunamis?

Undersea earthquakes create big swells. Meteor impacts create mammoth swells. Any questions?

SURF'S UP *This surfer's delight, a normal wave, curls up and goes tubular. In contrast, tsunami waves ripple quietly through the open sea, building height and speed when they reach the ascending land near the shore*

DO THE MATH," STEVEN WARD, A GEO-physicist at the University of California at Santa Cruz, told TIME in 2006. "We know of 160 major impact craters on land. Because almost three-quarters of Earth's surface is covered with water, it's likely that about three times that many have landed in the oceans." What happens when big meteors splash into the ocean is a professional preoccupation of Ward's, who has done extensive research into the effects of such a collision. "They're called megatsunamis," Ward said of the huge waves that would radiate outward from such a contact. "They could dwarf any wave in recorded human history—larger and more powerful than the Indian Ocean tsunami of 2004 by several orders of magnitude."

The difference between a tsunami caused by an earthquake and one caused by an asteroid impact is the amount of force behind each. "Although the energy released by a big quake is enormous," Ward said, "earthquakes can get only so big. There's a finite amount of energy trapped in the rock beneath the surface, and there are limits to how much it can build up before the rocks move and that energy is released. These limits carry over to the tsunamis that are sometimes created by large quakes."

But the limits don't apply to tsunamis created by asteroid impacts. "Throughout its history, Earth has been hit by asteroids at least one mile in diameter once every 100 million years or so. But even a relatively small space rock can have enormous consequences," Ward noted. As an example, he points to projections he has done for asteroid 1950 DA, a chunk of rock and metal slightly more than half a mile in diameter. "The best estimates give 1950 DA a one-third of 1% chance of hitting Earth on its next flyby. We know that the Atlantic Ocean will be facing the asteroid on that date. If it smashes into the Atlantic, it will be traveling at 38,000 m.p.h. The asteroid would vaporize on impact, but the blast would be the equivalent of 60,000 megatons." That translates into more than 4 million Hiroshima-type atom bombs being detonated all at once.

"The force would blow a hole in the ocean," Ward predicted, "which would then be filled by water rushing back into the void. The turbulence would oscillate a few times, then send shock waves radiating outward. We could expect that waves up to 400 ft. tall [122 m] would reach the U.S. coastline about two hours later. These waves would engulf everything from Massachusetts to North Carolina, and would probably penetrate about two miles past the shoreline." According to Ward's projections, smaller—but still devastating—tsunami waves would reach the coasts of Britain, France, Spain and Portugal about an hour later. In total, the lives of more than 120 million people would be at risk.

The good news: 1950 DA's next flyby isn't scheduled until March 16, 2880. "So we have plenty of time to prepare," Ward said. The bad news: there are many other dangerous asteroids lurking near Earth that we have not yet detected. Asked what can be done to prepare, the geophysicist noted, "For the distant future, there is reason to hope that we'll have the technology to divert asteroids. But in the meantime, the best thing we can do is to build bigger, better telescopes. And more of them." ∎

MUMBAI, INDIA *An umbrella comes with the territory on the Indian subcontinent, where residents strolled through the flooded streets of Mumbai in 1980*

Kingdoms Of Rain

Monsoon season brings life—and death—to the Indian subcontinent

AS SIBERIANS KNOW COLD AND BEDOUins know heat, Indians know rain. The Indian subcontinent is the home of one of the globe's most predictable weather patterns, an annual, months-long immersion in wind-borne rains known as monsoon season. The term was borrowed from Arab mariners who called the weather pattern the *mawsim,* or season of winds. To scientists, the annual event is a matter of cause and effect, the result of India's landmass growing hotter than the surrounding Indian Ocean in the summer, causing air masses over the land to rise and creating a low-pressure area beneath them, which breeds constant winds that blow moist ocean air onto the land. Translation: it rains a lot.

Monsoon seasons are found across the globe. Residents of the U.S. Southwest experience a summer monsoon season; Australia and southern Asia expect annual rains from a weather pattern known as the northeastern winter monsoon. Yet in India the monsoon season is far more than a matter of hot air and low-pressure zones; it is part of the rhythm of life. The winds and rain are cleansers, washing away a year's woes even as they cause inconvenience and disruption. They are an annual confirmation that all is right—and perilous—with the world. Indians anticipate the first drops of monsoon rain, which usually roll in right on time, punctual as a commuter train. The rains are expected to begin falling on the Andaman and Nicobar island chains in the Bay of Bengal on May 29. They make landfall at Kerala on June 1. Eight days later, they sweep into Mumbai, the nation's largest city and financial hub, and by the beginning of August the entire nation is subject to the reign of the rain. Meanwhile Cherrapunji and Mawsynram, a pair of cities in the Indian state of Meghalaya, vie for the honor of being the world's rainiest town.

Yet the rains can bring death as well as life. In 2010 a heavier-than-usual monsoon season spawned devastating floods in Pakistan, where some 2,000 people died, millions were left homeless, crops were ruined, and infrastructure was destroyed as the waters advanced. ■

Irresistible Force, Movable Objects

Floods can turn mankind's creations into kingdoms of muck

MAY 31, 1889. ANNA FENN, MOTHER of seven children and pregnant with an eighth, clings to her baby in her rapidly flooding home in Johnstown, Pa., while the other children grab onto any handhold they can find. Moments before, their father had been swept away by a wall of water 40 ft. (12 m) high and half a mile wide, roiling with human bodies, horses, debris and timber, when the Conemaugh River rampaged through the narrow valley where the town was perched. As Fenn would later write of her ordeal, "The water rose and floated us until our heads nearly touched the ceiling … It was dark and the house was tossing every way. The air was stifling, and I could not tell just the moment the rest of the children had to give up and drown … what I suffered, with the bodies of my seven children floating around me in the gloom, can never be told." She survived and gave birth weeks later; the infant did not live.

Aug. 29, 2005. In Biloxi, Miss., Phillip Bullard, 13, is trapped in an upper room of his home with a dozen other members of his family as floodwaters driven by Hurricane Katrina's big storm surge rise through the floorboards. Determined to take action, the youngster swims underwater to a submerged window that affords him an outlet. Returning first for his sister and stationing her safely outside, above the waters, he swims back into the house seven times, until every member of the family, including his mother, grandmother, twin sister and 1-year-old sister, is safe.

As these two tales illustrate, more than a century of spectacular technological advancement in design, engineering and building makes little difference when measured against the inexorable power of vast expanses of water in motion: a flood can reduce human life to a primal struggle for survival. Since the archetype of the beast—the biblical deluge Noah rode out in the ark—flooding has been one of humanity's central plagues.

Hurricanes and tornadoes may make more noise, and the symmetries of their cloud formations may be more fearsome, but flash floods are the No. 1 weather-related killer in the U.S.. Major floods like the Mississippi River catastrophes of 1927 and 1993 are the result of months of above-average precipitation, yet just as deadly are flash floods: smaller, often highly localized events that occur when heavy rains drop inches of water on a region whose topography does not offer sufficient runoff. Result: creeks, streets and low-water bridges can be inundated, and pedestrians and drivers are all too often swept away. According to the National Oceanic and Atmospheric Administration, floods claim an average of 100 lives and cause $2 billion in damages each year in the U.S.

Yet, like wildfires, floods play an essential role in nature's balance: the work of floodwaters created the Mississippi Delta and nourished the great civilizations of ancient Egypt. After all, when the angry God of the Old Testament brought an end to the 40-day deluge that swamped Noah's world, he signed his labors, and his new covenant with mankind, with a rainbow. ■

NEW ORLEANS, 2005 *Hurricane Katrina's storm surge, top, breached the city's low-lying levees, swamping streets, houses and entire wards of the Crescent City*

JOHNSTOWN, PA., 1889 *America's most memorable flood, near left, claimed some 2,200 victims when a rickety dam holding back the waters of a high-ground lake gave way, sending a cascade of water to join swollen rivers as they roared down a narrow valley and swamped the city*

MISSISSIPPI RIVER VALLEY, 1927 *After heavy rains, far right, soaked the big river's drainage basin, the river rose to unprecedented heights. When hastily built levees failed, flooding inundated 27,000 sq. mi. of land. Some 700,000 people were displaced; historians trace the Great Migration of Southern blacks to Northern cities to this epochal event*

From Ice To Water

As glaciers retreat and ice shelves break up, scientists try to measure the speed of polar melting

THE QUESTION ADDRESSES ONE OF THE most significant issues facing climate scientists today: How vulnerable are the vast ice caps of Greenland and Antarctica to rising temperatures? An unfathomable amount of ice is stored on those two landmasses, and as that ice melts and flows into the oceans, global sea levels rise—if all the ice on Greenland melted tomorrow, it would raise global sea levels by more than 20 ft. (6 m), swamping coastal cities and threatening millions worldwide. (The sea ice over the North Pole is melting too, and quickly, but since it's already in the water, the change doesn't raise sea levels any more than an ice-cube melting in a gin-and-tonic raises the level of the drink.)

Scientists agree that the planet's frozen zones are imperiled. Since the late 1990s, vast icebergs, many of them the size of U.S. states, have been breaking off from the South Pole and wandering into the Southern Ocean. In 2000, a 170-mile- (274 km) long chunk of ice dubbed B15 broke free of Antarctica's Ross Ice Shelf. Forcing alterations in the sea lanes to the scientific outpost at McMurdo Station, it roamed the waters around the South Pole for five years—the largest moving object on the planet. While the calving of such huge icebergs is part of the natural process at the poles, the size of the recent breakaway units has focused scientific attention on them.

Why are the ice caps breaking up? Global warming is the chief suspect, although the mechanisms driving the process remain unclear. Scientists warn that the world's glaciers, which cover about 10% of the planet's surface, could theoretically cause sea levels to rise more than 200 ft. (61 m), if they were all to melt down entirely.

ANTARCTICA *Penguins in the southern polar region are imperiled as ongoing melting of ice threatens their habitat*

More realistically, even a partial liquidation of the planet's glacial ice cover could have catastrophic consequences. And this frightening possibility may be on the horizon. Around 50 years ago, most glaciers near the poles were growing slowly but steadily. But in recent years, this pattern has been reversed, and many glaciers (both at the North and South poles) are retreating and melting. A study published in April 2005 by the British Antarctic Survey documented that the Sjogren Glacier near the South Pole has retreated more than eight miles (12.8 km) since 1993. Another 2005 study, by the U.S. National Science Foundation's Arctic System Science Program, concluded that within a century, the oceans around the North Pole may be ice free during the summer for the first time in a million years. The same study warned that as permafrost, the perpetually icy soil near the poles, begins to melt, the process may release vast amounts of methane and other greenhouse gases, possibly accelerating global climate change.

Getting a proper fix on how quickly polar land ice is melting would help scientists better model how quickly sea levels could rise in a warmer world—and that information would be vital for policymakers trying to respond to climate change. But the dynamics of the Greenland and Antarctic ice sheets are very complex—so much so that scientists at the Intergovernmental Panel on Climate Change decided not to try to calculate the potential increase in melt rate for those ice caps when it was estimating sea level rise for the next century. Nor does it help that carrying out science in these parts of the world is difficult, expensive—and cold.

Still, over the past several years scientists have been able to use data from NASA's twin Gravity Recovery and Climate Experiment (GRACE) satellites to begin to get better estimates of just how fast we're losing polar ice. (Changes in the mass of polar ice can actually affect Earth's gravitational field, and the GRACE satellites can detect those changes and use them to help calculate ice loss.) In recent years, studies using GRACE data estimated that Greenland was losing around 230 billion metric tons of ice a year, while West Antarctica was losing around 132 billion metric tons a year. Together that would account for 0.2 in. of sea level rise a year—which might seem like a small figure, but it's far higher than the 0.07 in. that seas rose annually in the 1960s.

Those are scary numbers, but a study published in the September 2010 issue of *Nature Geoscience* suggested that the true melt rate might be much slower than that. A joint team of American and Dutch scientists took another look at the GRACE data and found that Greenland and West Antarctica may be melting just half as fast as the earlier studies estimated. Researcher Bert Vermeersen, a professor at Delft University of Technology in the

The Poles: Melting Down and Breaking Up

On Feb. 26, 2010, a team of French and Australian scientists reported news of a huge iceberg's collision with the Mertz Glacier on the eastern coast of Antarctica. A chunk of sea ice approximately the size of Luxembourg was gouged out. Owing in part to warming global temperatures, Antarctica is losing ice all the time—about 24 cu. mi. (100 cu km) worth each year—a development that is slowly but steadily raising global sea levels, and scientists are worried that any additional uptick in those temperatures could suddenly accelerate that vast melting.

However, the models indicate that most ice loss should be happening on the western edge of the continent, where it is warmer, not in the much cooler east. No doubt there are complicated scientific reasons for this, but as TIME science correspondent Bryan Walsh observed, it pretty much boils down to what one researcher told a reporter: "There are some crazy things going down in Antarctica."

TAYLOR DRY VALLEY, ANTARCTICA *A glacier spills from the polar ice cap into the valley; many glaciers near the South Pole are becoming smaller each year, but the exact rate of the meltdown remains unclear*

Netherlands, explained that the earlier estimates failed to account for glacial isostatic adjustment—the scientific term for the rebounding of the earth's crust after the end of the last Ice Age.

"A good analogy is that it's like a mattress after someone has been sleeping on it all night," Vermeersen said. The weight of the sleeper creates a hollow as the material compress downward and outward. When the person gets up, the mattress starts to recover. This movement, seen in close-up, is both upward and downward and also sideways too, as the decompressed material expands outward and pulls on adjacent stuffing.

Often ignored or considered a minor factor in previous research, postglacial rebound is important, the *Nature Geoscience* paper said. Vermeersen and his colleagues used ground-based GPS stations and sea floor pressure, along with GRACE data, to get a better sense of what's happening to the land in Greenland and Antarctica. They found that southern Greenland is actually subsiding, or falling, as it's pulled down by the rebound of land in North America, while West Antarctica is rising, but not as fast as earlier studies estimated. As a result, they estimated Greenland is losing around 104 billion metric tons of ice a year, while West Antarctica is losing around 64 billion tons a year.

Climate-change skeptics seized on the results as proof that concerns over melting polar ice are overblown. But the *Nature Geoscience* study won't be the final word on the subject. Its own estimates of ice loss came with significant uncertainty, and as David Bromwich of Ohio State University pointed out, the estimates in the study rely on data from a very small number of GPS sites, all of which are located on the edges of the ice sheets.

The *Nature Geoscience* study also doesn't change the essential fact that the planet is losing ice on a daily basis from Greenland and West Antarctica—168 billion metric tons is still a lot of water to be adding to the global seas each year. Most of all, the study underscores the need to keep researching the impact of warming on our polar regions, which is why scientists were pleased when NASA extended the GRACE mission through 2015.

Even as the debate over the rate of glacial melting escalated, scientists studying the history of the planet's ice ages discovered mineral evidence suggesting the possibility that ice sheets may respond dynamically to changes in temperature, forming and melting at rates much faster than previously thought. The findings suggest that polar melting could make the world's seas rise even more quickly than we expected—bad news for those who think there's plenty of time to adapt to a warmer world. ∎

MELTDOWN! ICE CAPS RETREAT UP NORTH

The Arctic is warming up even faster than scientists feared. That could spell doom for these polar bears—and all the others

As Global Warming Melts Polar Ice ...

Temperatures in winter are rising faster than those in summer—as much as 5F to 7F in Alaska and western Canada

Over the past three decades, sea ice in the Arctic Ocean has declined an average of 8% annually, exposing an area larger than Texas and Arizona combined. The effect is most dramatic in summer, when ice levels drop as much as 20%

Yearly change from average arctic temperature

3.6F — 2C
1.8 — 1
0 — 0
Average
-1.8 — -1

1900 '20 '40 '60 '80 2000

SEPTEMBER **1979** North America

Greenland

SEPTEMBER **2003**

THE IMPACT WILL BE FELT IN MANY WAYS

COASTAL AREAS
As protective sea ice disappears and permafrost underlying the land's surface softens, coastal erosion will speed up dramatically. Floods will inundate marshes and estuaries, damaging both human and animal habitats

ARCTIC POPULATIONS
Indigenous people from Alaska to Canada to Siberia rely on fish, polar bears, seals and caribou for food, clothing and trade. As warming imperils these animals, it also threatens a way of life that has been unchanged for centuries

VEGETATION
Rising temperatures will let forests expand north into areas that now support only scrubby flora. Trees absorb more heat than bushes, speeding up local warming. Loss of tundra will also rob many animals of breeding and feeding grounds

WILDLIFE
Seals rest and give birth on sea ice; polar bears use it to stalk seals. Loss of ice will threaten both. On land, disruption of nesting areas could reduce populations of some migratory birds as much as 50% by the year 2100

WHY THE ARCTIC WARMS QUICKLY

There are many reasons. A key one: as ice melts, darker seawater and exposed land reflect less of the sun's energy, making the remaining ice melt even faster

20%
Reflected by vegetation and dark soil

Ice caps

Glacier

Lake ice

85%
Reflected by ice

Sea ice

10%
Reflected by ocean water

POLAR BEARS
Some 23,000 of these magnificent predators roam the Arctic today. By 2100 dwindling ice could wipe them out

... Rising Sea Levels May Inundate Coastlines

Sea level is expected to climb from 4 in. to 3 ft. by 2100, mainly from expanded warmer water and melting glaciers

Projected global sea-level rise under different emission scenarios

30 in.
20
10
0

80 cm
60
40
20
0

2000 '20 '40 '60 '80 2100

If the Greenland ice sheet melts, the effects of arctic warming could be especially damaging in low-lying places like Florida

Orlando

Tampa

Areas subject to inundation with a 3.3-ft. sea-level rise

West Palm Beach

Fort Myers

Miami

BUT IS IT ALL BAD?

NEW SEA ROUTES
A drastic reduction in polar ice during summer months could open reliable shipping lanes along the northern coast of Russia and Canada, making transportation cheaper and increasing access to oil. But there might also be more icebergs, which could limit the effectiveness of arctic shipping

Northern sea route

Northwest Passage

2010-2030

Ice extent September 2002

2040-2060

Ice extent 2070-2090

OTHER ADVANTAGES
Some species may actually benefit from global warming. Cod and arctic char, both commercially important fish, could expand their range. Some crops, including barley and alfafa, could be grown in areas that are too cold today

Text by Kristina Dell
Source: Arctic Climate Impact Assessment Maps: Clifford Grabhorn

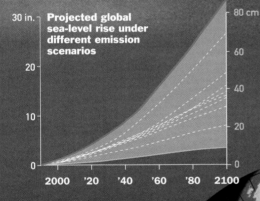

The recipe for creating land staggers the mind. The stuff that composes the planet's surface is cooked up in the heated realms beneath the earth's crust and expelled as lava through fiery volcanoes. Then it is further shaped, riven by tectonic fault lines, scoured by glaciers and winds. After the land stews for 20 or 40 centuries in local climatic conditions, the result is what scientists call a biome, an environment conducive to the growth of specific plants and animals: a desert or a rain forest or a vast tundra. The end? No. There's no stopping nature's works upon the globe, but they take place on a timetable far too expansive for our eyes to see. Yet in recent centuries, a new force—humanity—has entered the equation, and now a power other than nature is helping shape the planet. But no wise person doubts which is the superior partner.

THE LAND PLANET

NASA—GSFC—METI—ERSDAC—JAROS, AND U.S.—JAPAN ASTER SCIENCE TEAM

PAYSON, ARIZ., 2004 *This false-color infrared image, taken from a satellite, shows the Willow wildfire burning on July 3. Scorched areas show up as magenta, active fires are darker red, vegetation is green, and smoke is blue*

A Movable Feast

ARCTIC NATIONAL WILDLIFE REFUGE, ALASKA In this federally protected preserve, some of the estimated 123,000 caribou of the Porcupine herd are moving north and east toward their annual calving grounds near the Beaufort Sea. The areas of the planet that support life, the biomes, are divided into five major areas: aquatic, deserts, tundra, forests and grasslands. Tundra features a very cold climate, a short growing season, simple vegetation and the presence of only a few types of animals, most of which, like the caribou, migrate each year.

MICHIO HOSHINO / MINDEN PICTURES

There Goes the Neighborhood

LAGUNA BEACH, CALIF. This house, built on hilly terrain, was one of several million-dollar homes that lost their footings and were carried downhill when a landslide rocked Bluebird Canyon, an exclusive enclave along the Pacific Coast, on June 1, 2005. Scientists traced the event to heavy rains earlier in the year. "It was like something out of a movie," resident Ryan Haskell told reporters, recalling how his home was lost. "Our only recourse was to run down the canyon as the houses were sliding around us." Fortunately, no lives were lost.

A Lake for Old Salts

LAKE NATRON, TANZANIA Located in the Great Rift Valley of East Africa, a convergence zone of tectonic plates, Lake Natron contains large volumes of volcanic ash produced by eons of eruptions. Like Utah's Great Salt Lake, this is an alkaline body of water but even saltier. Its waters are coated in a thin crust tinted red by multitudes of *Spirulina*—blue-green algae, colored with red pigments—that feed off its salt. The algae are in turn fodder for the lesser flamingo, whose pink-tinged feathers reflect the algae's pigment.

GERRY ELLIS—MINDEN PICTURES

Torrents Of Slime

When rain turns hilly soil to mud, gravity becomes the enemy

AS TROPICAL STORMS GO, JOSÉ WAS not especially big. Yet it turned out to be a killer, just the same. The low-pressure system left the coast of Africa on Aug. 8, 2005, and its clouds bulked up a bit on the warm waters of the Caribbean Sea. By the time its leading edge approached Mexico's Yucatán Peninsula on Aug. 22, it had attained sufficient strength to be designated a tropical storm and christened José by the National Hurricane Center in Miami. José never grew to hurricane strength, however: when it made landfall in Mexico, it lacked the strong winds that are the howling signature of a hurricane. But José dumped as much as 10 in. (25 cm) of rain on the region in a 24-hr. period—and that was enough to trigger massive mudslides in the area's hilly terrain. By the time José broke up and entered the record books as just another routine, short-lived storm, the huge cascades of mud unleashed by its rains had left six people dead and thousands homeless.

If deadly José was a relatively minor event, consider a real killer, 2005's Hurricane Stan. Like José, Stan was described as a rather weak storm. But Stan's clouds, in tandem with a larger rainstorm system of which it was a part, dumped some 20 in. (50 cm) of rain across portions of Mexico and Central America early in October. The deluge set off monster mudslides all around the region. The

PANABAJ, GUATEMALA, 2005 *A woman surveys the devastation that resulted when much of the town was inundated by sludge*

LEFT: DANIEL AGUILAR—REUTERS—CORBIS; RIGHT: LOPEZ—EL DIARIO DE HOY—GAMMA

EL SALVADOR, 2001
An earthquake triggered a mudslide here that cut a swath through the hilly terrain of La Colina de Santa Tecla. In all, 844 people died

ARMERO, COLOMBIA, 1985 *Much of the town was buried by the mudslide. Below, rescuers could not free Omaira Sanchez, trapped when the town was hit, and she died*

worst tragedies afflicted Panabaj, a poor village perched precariously on the slopes near Lake Atitlán in Guatemala's Sololá department, and Piedra Grande, a small town in the municipality of San Pedro Sacatepéquez. Both hamlets were essentially buried in mud, not so much wiped off the face of the earth as absorbed into it. The towns are now considered graveyards; in Piedra Grande some 1,400 people were buried alive.

Even Hurricane Stan's death count pales when compared with the calamity that struck the nation of Colombia in 1985. In one of the great natural disasters of the 20th century, the long-dormant volcano Nevado del Ruiz suddenly came alive on Nov. 13. Within hours, its rebirth left upwards of 23,000 people buried in a steaming, mile-wide avalanche of mud and ash that swept down the slopes of the 17,716-ft. (5.4 km) mountain. The town of Armero (est. pop. about 22,500) essentially disappeared, along with the majority of its inhabitants.

Nevado del Ruiz did not produce the spectacular lava displays we associate with eruptions. Instead, the tragedy began when superheated magma within its cone began to melt the thick blanket of snow and ice that capped the uppermost 2,000 ft. (609 m) of the peak. Filthy water started to flow down the sides of the mountain. The trickle swiftly turned into a torrent of viscous mud, stone, ash and debris, cresting between 15 and 50 ft (4.5-15 m). The liquid avalanche, or lahar, was soon hurtling down the steep slopes at speeds of up to 30 m.p.h., following the riverbeds that channel water from the peak.

In Armero, as survivor Rosa Maria Henao, then 39, told TIME later, the mudslide "rolled into town with a moaning sound, like some sort of monster. Houses below us started cracking under the advance of the river of mud." Fortunately, her home was on relatively high ground; Henao grabbed her two children and sought refuge on its roof. As they watched, more than 80% of the roughly 4,200 buildings in Armero simply vanished in the mud.

Survivors testified that the first wave of mud to hit the town was ice cold, like the mountain snows that spawned it. Only later did the cascade turn smoking hot, as lava from the volcano caught up with the mudslide it had unleashed. Armero, in Henao's words, was now "one big beach of mud." A viscous gray layer, between 7 and 15 ft. thick, covered most of the town. Thousands of bodies were buried deep in the sludge, their location sometimes marked by pools of blood on the surface. Some survivors were naked or only partly clothed; their garments had been torn from them by the swift-moving lahar. All were encrusted with ash-colored goo that quickly hardened under the next morning's sun into a gritty carapace.

Most horrifying of all was the plight of those who were trapped, still living, in the mud. Many were buried up to their necks; some had their mouths stopped with filth, so they could not cry for help. Sometimes the buried survivors were still locked in gruesome embrace with the dead. One was Omaira Sanchez, 13, who remained up to her neck in ooze two days after the disaster. When the mudslide struck, she was washed up against her aunt, who grabbed hold of her. The aunt died but kept her grip, even after rigor mortis had set in. Finally, after rescuers had toiled for 60 hours, Sanchez died of a heart attack. One doctor estimated that there were at least 1,000 living victims trapped in the morass; few escaped with their lives.

The science of landslides is not esoteric; they are essentially a marriage of gravity and mud. But today scientists are beginning to implicate landslides in a different kind of disaster, as they explore the possibility that undersea landslides can either cause tsunamis or heighten the effects of one caused by an undersea earthquake. After a magnitude-7 earthquake on July 7, 1998, giant waves swamped beaches on the north coast of Papua New Guinea, killing more than 2,200 people on the island.

As scientists from the National Oceanic and Atmospheric Administration reviewed the event, they were puzzled by the fact that not only was the wave larger than predicted by models for an earthquake that size but also that it arrived some 10 minutes later than expected. Explorations of the undersea earthquake site by manned submersibles found evidence that the big wave may have been triggered by the slump of a slope of seafloor perched on unstable ground. The research suggests that in this case the term landslide may be a misnomer; this deadly process originated miles from the sight of land. ∎

White Death

Snow symbolizes purity and renewal—most of the time

WHY DO AVALANCHES SEEM MORE appalling and less explicable than other natural disasters? One reason is that they occur in mountainous regions, areas that take us close to the heavens, where the air is thin and all seems pure. Another is that their occurrence is so unpredictable as to seem whimsical. But surely the main reason is because an avalanche is a killer dressed in white, and we are raised to believe that bad guys wear black.

Skiers and snowboarders know better. Avalanches— swift, powerful, silent and deadly—are their greatest enemy. Torrents of sliding snow claim some 150 lives across the planet each year, and that number is rising, not falling, as skiing, snowmobiling and other winter sports attract ever more enthusiasts. But avalanches are indiscriminate, striking the poor as well as the wealthy: on Feb. 17, 2010, an avalanche fueled by heavy snowfalls struck several towns in Badakhshan Province in eastern Pakistan, killing as many as 100 people.

As with their ugly cousins, mudslides and landslides, avalanches are scientifically simple: the recipe calls for snow, slopes, mass and gravity. The problem: there's often a lot of mass involved. A typical U.S. avalanche might release 250,000 to 350,000 cu. yds. of snow, enough to fill, well, a very long line of dump trucks. Scientists divide the event into three stages, beginning with the topmost section, the starting zone. The trouble begins when unstable snow splits off from the main snowpack and starts to slide. The second section is the avalanche track, the path the snow follows until it reaches a stop in the third stage, the runout zone.

Skiers, hikers and snowmobilers: listen for a hollow *whump* sound as you pass over sloping snow. That's the telltale sign of an unstable snowpack that may be ready to start slipping. There's time to get away—a little— before the peaceful mountain turns a whole lot less so. ∎

ZURS, AUSTRIA *Snow cascades into the ski resort in February 1999, when heavy snowfalls fueled Alpine avalanches. Another slide in Austria that month killed 38 skiers*

Paradise Lost

Imperiled rain forests are the planet's lungs and hothouses for new species

BACK IN THE EARLY 1990S, I WAS CATA-loging plant species in the Colombian rain forest," Cristián Samper, the noted biologist who is the director of the Smithsonian Institution's National Museum of Natural History, told TIME in 2006. "I had been there for several days when a colleague and I came upon a stunning flower that was like nothing we had ever seen before. It was bright orange and had long, beautiful petals. We took it back to the taxonomists, who realized that this was an entirely new species of flower in the family *Gesneriaceae*. They eventually called it *Sinningia elatior*."

Such moments of discovery have enchanted and inspired the native Colombian since he was a teenager. Samper began collecting rare plants and insects as a boy and embarked on his first scientific trek into the Amazon rain forest at age 15. He believes there is far more at stake

in identifying new species of flora and fauna than the thrill of discovery.

"Plants and animals are always engaged in what we call a 'co-evolutionary arms race,'" Samper said. "Unlike animals, plants can't run away from the things that eat them. So they have to devise chemical defenses against animals, diseases and other plants." This treasure trove of natural chemical innovation explains why one-quarter of all prescription drugs are derived from plants. "The competition among plants and between plants and animals," Samper continued, "is the most intense where the greatest number of them live." As it happens, more than 50% of all animal species on the planet—and more than 66% of all varieties of plant life—inhabit only 2% percent of its surface: Earth's lush, densely overgrown rain forests.

Scientists say there is every reason to suspect that there are hundreds, perhaps thousands, of miracle drugs hid-

BRAZIL'S RAIN FORESTS *The forest is preserved at the nation's Serra de Bocaina National Park, left, while slash-and-burn agriculture takes its toll in the state of Roraima, right*

den beneath the canopies of the world's rain forests. They remain undiscovered only because the rain forests themselves are largely unexplored. "We just don't know about most of the living things inside of rain forests," Samper said. "Some estimates are that we have cataloged as few as 10% of the plants and mosses and have overlooked more than one-third of all the animals." We do know that fewer than 1% of all the plants so far identified have been tested for medicinal properties. Of these, according to the Nature Conservancy, more than 2,000 have been demonstrated to have potential in fighting cancer, while many more show promise as therapies against other diseases.

Sadly, the hidden bounties of these exotic woodlands may be lost forever, because the rain forests are disappearing. Paleontologists estimate that the ancient world contained more than 6 million sq. mi. of rain forest. Much less than half of those forests remains—and about a quarter of the original amount has been cleared in the past 200 years. Large forests in India, Sri Lanka, Bangladesh and Haiti have been lost entirely, while those in West Africa and South America are shrinking rapidly.

As the forests are slashed and burned, the life within them also goes up in smoke. The consensus among biologists is that more than 50 different species of plants and animals are becoming extinct within the world's forests every 24 hours. That far exceeds the rate at which new species are developing, and amounts to the greatest die-off since the dinosaurs became extinct.

It is possible that human life depends on species we have not yet discovered and systems we do not yet understand. "We are taught to think of food as a chain," Samper explained, "with microbes at the bottom, plants and animals in the middle and human beings at the top. But it's really much more like a web, where every strand supports and relies upon every other strand. If you put stress on any segment, it will be felt all across the web. Take away even one strand, and the whole web gets weaker. If you

99

take away more than a few, the entire web may collapse."

That web has already collapsed for millions of human beings. Historians estimate that before the year 1500, there were some 6 million indigenous tribespeople living in the Brazilian Amazon. By the first decade of the 20th century, fewer than 250,000 remained. Even today, previously unknown cultures are being discovered deep within the jungle, as miners and timber companies cut new roads into unexplored ground. Many tribes vanish within a few decades of their first contact with the outside world.

Because many of the nations with the largest rain forests are underdeveloped, and their resources are untapped, the forests are particularly rich, tempting assets. The timber there is heavily weighted toward valuable teak, sandalwood, mahogany, rosewood and balsa. Once these trees have been felled and cleared, the soil exposed is enormously fertile, making it ideal for agriculture. These opportunities translate into a devastating one-two punch in which valuable timber is clear-cut to make way for farming or grazing. But the benefit seldom lasts: after the rain forest's protective ecosystem has been erased, the soil often degrades quickly or is eroded away. Within a few years the farmers and ranchers move on to the next swath of recently cleared rain forest acreage, leaving a wasteland behind them.

Rain forests are not only hothouses of biological diversity; they are also the lungs of the planet, in ways we are only beginning to measure. Because their vegetation vacuums up carbon dioxide and expels oxygen, rain for-

VANISHING
Fleischmann's glass frogs

LA PLANADA, COLOMBIA
Cristián Samper examines the initial descending root of a Clusia *hemiepiphyte in the rain forest canopy*

The Vanishing Tropical Frogs

THEY SEEM HARDY, but frogs are actually frail beings, with a semipermeable skin that leaves them vulnerable to the slightest hiccup in their environment. So when entire species of harlequin frogs, like the flying tree harlequin frog below, started dying off in the cloud forests of Central and South America 30 years ago, scientists knew there was trouble in those ecosystems.

In January 2006 scientists compared changes in annual forest temperatures with the number of frog species seen. The results, report-ed in the science journal *Nature,* documented for the first time a direct correlation between global warming and the extinction of about two-thirds of the 110 known species of harlequin frogs. Data collected in Costa Rica showed that species die-offs follow warm years 80% of the time. It's not heat alone that kills harlequins: a fungus that attacks their skin thrives in cool weather—and global warming leads to cloudier, cooler days in the frogs' forest home.

ests help mitigate the effects of greenhouse gases and slow down global warming. Since they collect and concentrate humidity, the forests also help regulate temperature—not just locally, but globally.

Nothing infuriates the residents of these critical regions more than the notion that richer nations are entitled to a say in how their forests are managed. But the rest of the world does have a significant stake in the future of the forests. As a result of widespread burning to clear the land for agriculture, some scientists now worry that major rain forests, like those in the Amazon, may soon become net contributors of carbon dioxide and other greenhouse gases to the atmosphere. "The consequences of deforestation are almost incalculable," Samper said. "Locally, they include flooding and loss of topsoil. But defor-

estation also contributes to climate change, which means that people in Africa may be affected by the loss of rain forest in the Amazon basin.

"Two years after the expedition in which we discovered the new species of *Gesneriaceae,*" Samper recalled, "I went back to the same place in Colombia. We found that the forest where we had been working was gone. It had been burned and cleared. No other specimens of *Sinningia elatior* have ever been found. As far as we know, it is now extinct." Asked whether that plant might have held promise as a new medicine or perhaps helped another species of plant or animal survive, he shrugs and answers, "We'll probably never know." What we do know is that there are only so many fertile spots we can burn or clear before the last of them is gone. ■

101

In the Line Of Fire

They take a terrible toll, yet wildfires are a necessary scourge

THE DATE WAS JAN. 1, 2006, BUT MANY residents of Oklahoma had no time to celebrate the new year: they were busy fighting to save their homes, farms and cattle, imperiled by some of the largest wildfires ever to afflict the state. Aided and abetted by a trio of contributing factors—abnormally high winter temperatures, consistently low rainfall and steady high winds—wildfires raced across the state's dry, grassy plains beginning in November 2005. By Jan. 3, after most of the flames were finally extinguished, four people were dead, more than 250 homes and buildings had burned to the ground, and some 331,000 acres of grasslands had been consumed. At

the same time, fires were also rampaging through neighboring Texas. Governor Rick Perry, describing the parched plains of the Lone Star State as "a tinderbox," declared the entire state a disaster area.

Ten days after the first wave of fires was quelled, a fresh batch swept across Oklahoma, destroying at least 24 homes and forcing hundreds of people to evacuate. At the ranch of Gayla Stacy, 53, about 60 miles south of Oklahoma City, flames burned down the barn, destroyed farm equipment and consumed 160 acres of land where her 150 head of cattle grazed. Also lost: more than 100 rolls of hay set aside for winter feed. "We've worked 35 years to get what we've got, and we're glad our house didn't burn, but it still hurts," Stacy told CBS News. "It's knocked a big hole in our livelihood." Meanwhile, Oklahoma Governor Brad Henry canceled a planned helicopter tour of the devastated area so the state chopper could be put to a more urgent use: it was enlisted in the battle against the spreading flames.

A tragedy? Yes. Yet wildfires cannot simply be branded as one of nature's plagues. Like the Roman god Janus, wildfires wear two faces. However bitter the toll they take on forests, plains and farms in the short run, their flames are essential to the planet's balance over the long haul, playing a critical role in the cycle of natural renewal, re-

The fires in Oklahoma and Texas were a by-product of weather conditions, but even dry grass needs a spark to combust: the most common culprits include lightning, human carelessness and, sadly, arson. According to the scientists at the Maine Forest Service, arsonists cause 1 out of every 4 wildfires in the state. Americans were stunned in 2002 when Terry Lynn Barton, a U.S. Forest Service employee, pleaded guilty to having started the largest wildfire in Colorado history, the Hayman blaze, which consumed 138,000 acres southwest of Denver, destroying 133 homes and causing an estimated $13 million in damages. Barton, then 38, faced both state and federal

At a time when global temperatures have been steadily ticking upward, wildfires promise to become a larger threat to mankind. Two major events in recent years offered a dire preview of the future. In January and February 2009, summer in the southern hemisphere, Australia suffered the worst bushfires, as they're called Down Under, in the nation's history. Powered by a heat wave and high, dry winds, bushfires raged across southeastern Australia for weeks, killing more than 170 people, injuring more than 400 others, burning more than 2,000 houses to the ground and leaving more than 7,000 people homeless. Most of the fires were started by natural causes, but in one case, a former volunteer firefighter, Brendan James Sokaluk, then 39, was arrested and charged with arson causing death. As of early 2011, his case had yet to come to trial.

In 2010 Russia experienced its hottest summer on record, and by early August some 500 major wildfires were raging across the vast nation. In addition to the damage the fires wrought on farms and communities, where as many as 100 people died, the big fires created a calamity in the form of a toxic smog that descended upon Moscow and other cities: by one estimate, more than 50,000 people suffering from respiratory conditions died.

For much of the 20th century, wildfires were seen as a blight and nothing more. The lesson was drilled into generations of children by the plight of the animated forest animals that fled raging flames in Walt Disney's *Bambi*. Meanwhile, kids learned that "only you can prevent forest fires," courtesy of beloved U.S. Forest Service spokesbear, Smokey. Beginning in the 1960s, however, scientists began to change their tune, realizing that wildfires are essential to the long-term health of forests and prairies.

That knowledge doesn't make conditions any easier for those whose homes and lives are challenged by fire. And those numbers are increasing, as more people build residences in known wildfire areas. The conflagrations that devastated Southern California in October 2003 are all too typical of the sorrows wildfires can sow. In Wynola, 40 miles northeast of San Diego, a firefighter trying to save a house died when a freak turn of wind blew the fire in his direction; the colleague who tried to save him sustained burns over 20% of his body. Some people were luckier. A couple in one subdivision rode out the fire by diving into their swimming pool as the windows of their house exploded.

One of the worst natural disasters in California history, the infernos enveloped more than 750,000 acres, killed 20 people and destroyed nearly 3,000 houses. Yet these were disasters foretold, the tragic but predictable result of the push of people and dwellings into forests and brushlands designed by nature to burn.

As Duke University fire ecologist Norm Christensen explained to TIME, wildfires have been erupting in the canyons and foothills of California's coastal mountains for thousands of years. The recipe to produce them: take a tract of pine and fir trees or shrubby chaparral. Watch the trees grow for several decades. Then wait for the

SAN DIEGO, 2003 *The Cedar wildfire threatens the Scripps Ranch subdivision, where hundreds of homes burned. A lost hunter confessed he*

winter rains to stop, so the tinder can dry, becoming a "fuel load" for fire. At that point, a spark is all it takes to start a conflagration. In 2003, only days after that first spark was struck, 14,000 firefighters found themselves arrayed along a chaotic front, often watching helplessly as flames engulfed houses and leaped across freeways.

Fires that occur in the zone where suburban sprawl abuts rugged, wild lands are known as intermix fires, and they are a firefighter's nightmare. Vastly complicating the ability to protect property and lives are nonnatural hazards like narrow, twisting roads that dead-end in blind canyons or houses with cedar-shake roofs and logs stacked beside the kitchen door. It's too late to prohibit developments that are in place, but the danger can still be mitigated. Adopting and enforcing more stringent building and landscaping codes, fire experts insist, are critical. California's Ventura County, for example, now requires 100-ft. (30 m) buffer zones between homes and surrounding wild lands.

The goal is to preserve nature's balance. According to Richard Minnich, a fire ecologist at the University of California at Riverside, it is the long history of wildfire suppression in the U.S. that has allowed fuel loads in so many areas to build to unprecedented levels. When we try to thwart nature's rhythms, it seems, we often wind up, quite literally, playing with fire. ∎

THE SCIENCE OF WILDFIRES

Wildfires exist in a world of their own, with their own dynamics and their own weather. Before you can fight a fire, you need to understand the forces that drive it. The lesson of these big blazes is that fire is a natural occurrence that we must learn to tolerate and even sometimes encourage

HOW THEY START

Wildfires result from a confluence of fuel, dryness and some kind of trigger. Each factor contributes to the severity of the blaze

■ **Fuel** means flammable solids—grass, pine needles, undergrowth, smaller trees—that, with oxygen, feed the fire

■ **Dryness** can be caused by short-term weather patterns with low humidity or by a lengthy drought that parches the landscape

■ **Triggers** can be as natural as a lightning strike, as innocent as a campfire or as sinister as an arsonist

HOW THEY SPREAD

Weather is the primary force that drives or contains wildfires. But once they start burning, they create their own weather

(1) **Smoke and heat** from fires can rise thousands of feet in the air

(2) Then **cooler air** rushes in to fill the void

(3) This convection system creates **gale-force hot winds** that dry out and preheat fuel ahead of the fire and can propel burning embers as much as half a mile (0.8 km)

HOW TO FIGHT THEM

A fire dies when it is deprived of fuel, heat or oxygen. The main strategy for fighting wildfires is containment: surround the fire and starve it

■ **Helicopters and tanker airplanes** can drop water or chemical retardants to slow the spread of flames

■ **Firefighters can set up fire lines,** areas cleared of any fuel that would allow the fire to spread

■ **Controlled fires** are sometimes set to deny fuel to an approaching blaze

(1) **Column of rising hot air creates a void below**

(2) **Fresh air rushes in, bringing more oxygen to fuel the flames**

(3) **Blowing embers allow the fire to jump natural barriers such as rivers and valleys**

WIND

WIND

FUEL

It's a dangerous recipe: decades of fighting every forest fire have left many areas dangerously full of fuel—sticks, fallen timber, pine needles and brush. Long-term droughts can sap the natural moisture from the ground

TORNADO WINDS

In rare cases, erratic winds within a wildfire create powerful mini-tornadoes that can shoot spirals of flame into the air and twist trees apart at their trunks

SOIL INSULATION

Soil is an excellent insulator that can protect tree roots from a fire's heat, permitting regrowth to begin quickly. But a charred landscape is also vulnerable to erosion

AND HOW TO DEAL WITH THEM

For much of the 20th century, Americans treated forest fires as anathema, to be stamped out wherever they occurred. But experts now believe the zero-tolerance approach did more harm than good.

Fires are part of the natural rhythm of the forests, clearing out underbrush and giving trees room to grow. You don't really fight wildfires, according to this view; you only postpone them. If we are going to learn how to coexist with fire, here is how we might start:

DON'T BUILD
Fire is part of the natural life of a forest, say environmentalists; vacation houses aren't. If you don't put them up, you won't have to save them

BUILD SMART
If you have to build, use fire-resistant materials and clear out any underbrush and other combustibles

LET IT BURN
Fires clean out the forest; let them do their job. With more people than ever living in fire-prone areas, however, that's a tough sell

PRESCRIPTION FIRES
Set controlled burns on purpose to clear away undergrowth. The risk is that they will burn out of control

CHANGE THE LANDSCAPE
To reduce fire risk, forests can be thinned by hand. Some experts advocate restoring grasslands that have been taken over by woody vegetation

TIME Graphic by Ed Gabel; reported by Laura Bradford and David Bjerklie

Sources: Greg Aplet, the Wilderness Society; Stephen Pyne, Arizona State University; William Romme, Colorado State University; AP; National Interagency Fire Center; U.S. Forest Service

RETARDANT

Nitrogen-heavy fertilizer mixed with water coats fuel to prevent burning. Iron oxide in the retardant gives it its orange color

UPHILL BATTLE

Wildfires charge rapidly up mountainsides because the heat from the fire rises and is directed at the fuel uphill, drying it out before the flames arrive

BACKFIRE

Backfires are another method of depriving a fire of fuel so that it burns itself out

(1) Using axes, chainsaws and bulldozers, firefighters create an area called a fire line that is free of all flammable materials

(2) Upwind of the fire line, a fire is started— usually in the morning or evening, when breezes are calmer—that burns parallel to the fire line

(3) Prevailing winds carry the backfire toward the fire line. Everything in between is burned, creating a wide, fuel-free barrier that, with luck, the approaching fire cannot cross

BACKFIRE

PREVAILING WIND

FIRE LINE

True Grit

The desert, my friend, is blowin' in the wind

MARCH 24, 2003: MORE THAN 167,000 American and British troops were waking up to the fourth day of Gulf War II. Invading Saddam Hussein's Iraq from the staging area in Kuwait in long convoys of armored vehicles, including tanks, artillery and personnel carriers, they were racing across the desert, hellbent for Baghdad. The spearhead of the forces, the U.S. Army's 3rd Infantry Division, was only 50 miles (80

km) outside the capital city—when suddenly the entire mammoth operation came to a grinding, clanking halt, throwing the Pentagon's carefully worked-out timetable off track. The long-awaited invasion had been put on hold, not by Iraq's military but by a haboob.

A what? Haboobs are the massive dust storms that blow for miles (and days) across deserts and dry regions, where sand and wind are plentiful but soil is scarce. Haboobs are commonplace in the Sahara, stirred up by

the region's strong sirocco winds, and they're also familiar to Americans who dwell in the desert Southwest. Haboobs can be generated by outflow winds, the horizontal, spreading downdrafts that precede thunderstorms, or they can occur when hot desert air rises and nearby lower, cooler winds rush into a region. Towering over the desert at heights that can reach 5,000 ft. (1,520 m), a haboob like the one that struck in Iraq in 2003 can cut off visibility completely, even as it fills every aperture it can find—a soldier's gun barrel, say, and his boots and his pack and his eyes—with fine, irritating grit.

More than just a nuisance, sandstorms and dust storms can kill livestock, disrupt communications systems and halt travel. Even worse, they can blow away topsoil essential to agriculture, as they did in the U.S. during the bitter years of the Dust Bowl in the 1930s. Yet sandstorms also play their part in the vast global chain of natural interdependence: some scientist believe such storms are part of the process by which essential minerals are borne by jet streams high across the Atlantic from Africa to the rain forests along the Amazon River. In recent years data returned by NASA probes revealed that huge sandstorms are a common feature of the climate on Mars: they put the red in the Red Planet. ∎

OMDURMAN, SUDAN, 2004 *A haboob swirls into a cattle market. The term is Arabic for, roughly, "violent wind"*

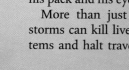

In the delicate natural web that supports life on Earth, one of the most essential ingredients is almost invisible: the atmosphere. The planet is swaddled in a cocoon of air, the realm of clouds and lightning, meteors and auroras, powerful winds and deadly tornadoes. As technology improves, our view of this elusive world becomes richer, more complex, more surprising. In the 20th century alone, we first saw hurricanes from above, first realized that giant jet streams channel winds high across the globe, first suspected that objects from far beyond our planet could some-day put an end to it. Even the sun, essential to life, bears danger: its giant flares can disrupt communications, shut down power grids, alter the weather. The ancients sensed that heavenly bodies ruled affairs on Planet Earth: that's why the study of weather is called meteorology.

ABOVE THE PLANET

ATLANTIC OCEAN *This false-color radar image, taken from a satellite in 1999, shows surface wind speeds on the sea; magenta and yellow tracks are faster, blue slower. Tropical Storm Harvey is the large swirling object in the Caribbean*

When Fear Comes In Spirals

NEWCASTLE, OKLA. There is no more frightening sight in the U.S. Midwest than the funnel-shaped cloud of a tornado. Above, Tammy Holmgren huddles beneath a highway overpass with her two daughters, Megan, 6, right, and Katlyn (partially obscured), 2, as a twister approaches on May 3, 1999. The Holmgrens escaped, but 44 other Oklahomans lost their lives when one of the largest storm systems ever recorded moved through the area, spawning 61 separate tornadoes.

J. PAT CARTER—AP IMAGES

Katrina: Ka-boom

KENNER, LA. When Hurricane Katrina made landfall in Louisiana, about 6:10 a.m. on Monday, Aug. 29, 2005, its winds were raging at some 125 m.p.h. Originally rated as a Category 4 storm, Katrina was later declared to have been a Category 3 storm at landfall. But whatever its rating, there is no doubt that its effects on the Gulf Coast were off the charts. Katrina devastated the historic Mississippi coastline, flooded and shut down New Orleans—and announced its arrival by ripping the roof right off a restaurant in nearby Kenner.

Nature's Light Show

PANAMA CITY, PANAMA For much of human history, lightning
was one of the least understood and, in a world built of wood,
most feared of weather phenomena. Big bolts like the one that
rocked Panama's capital in 2004 could set entire cities ablaze.
Benjamin Franklin's theory that lightning's force could be
channeled harmlessly into the ground via a metal rod was first
tested successfully by French scientists on May 10, 1752.
When the experiment proved his thesis to be valid, Franklin was
hailed as one of mankind's greatest scientific visionaries.

Storms on Steroids

Vast spirals of wind and water,
hurricanes are the planet's
deadliest weather system

KEY WEST, FLA. *Brian Goss, left, George Wallace and Michael Mooney battle 90-m.p.h. winds along Houseboat Row on Sept. 25, 1998. The three had sought shelter behind a hotel as Hurricane Georges hit the Keys, but they fled when the storm became too rough*

THE DATE WAS AUG. 28, 1992. AS HURRIcane Andrew's howling, 142-m.p.h. winds swirled around the home of Jo and Bruce Powers in Naranja, Fla., a Miami suburb, they hid with their two children, Jo's sister Karen Brocato and several neighbors in a couple of small bathrooms. For two hours Bruce braced his foot on the sink in one of them, wedging his 200-lb. frame against the door to keep the hurricane from ripping it open. The terrified group heard glass shatter and stick in the walls. Water poured in around the medicine chest, and

119

KATRINA, 2005 *When the storm breached New Orleans' levees, the city flooded, above, leading to a flurry of rescues, below*

the tub rattled itself away from the wall. Roof tiles flew under the door. "I've never been so scared in my life," Brocato told TIME a few days later. "I hope I die if I'm ever that afraid again. We all dirtied our pants."

A hurricane will do that to you. Of all nature's deadly extremes, these big storms seem the most personal. Landslides, floods, earthquakes and volcanoes are killers, yet they never seem more than the vast, impersonal rumblings of a living planet. But the big spiral storms seem to seek people out and test their mettle in personal combat: Andrew vs. Bruce Powers. Perhaps it all goes back to the 1950 decision by the U.S. Weather Bureau to begin publicly referring to the big storms by the alphabetical nicknames used informally by staff meteorologists. Suddenly hurricanes were no longer unknowable forces of nature but clearly identifiable villains: Camille and Frances, Ivan and Charley. Even reporters trained to avoid attributing human emotions to natural events commonly refer to

ANDREW, 1992 *Winds from the fourth most intense storm to make landfall in the U.S. in modern history tossed trucks like chaff*

"Andrew's fury," "Camille's malevolence" or "Katrina's wrath," and readers nod their heads.

Hurricanes, like people, wear shrouds of legend. In 1494 Christopher Columbus, on his second voyage to the Americas, became the first European to see a hurricane. Eight years later, on his fourth voyage, Columbus warned the Governor of Santo Domingo that a hurricane was approaching, but when his advice was ignored, a Spanish treasure fleet lost 20 ships and 500 men. Some 450 years later, U.S. Navy Admiral William (Bull) Halsey ran smack into a typhoon—the Pacific Ocean version of hurricanes—and lost three destroyers and 790 men. Neil Young writes songs about hurricanes; heavyweight boxers take nicknames from them; defiant New Orleanians christened a drink after them.

Scientists have learned much about hurricanes in the past 150 years. Today we know the big storm takes shape when large low-pressure systems draw in air and begin to spin in a counterclockwise direction, creating a spiral pattern around a central, calm eye. The storm's power is fed as its winds draw up warm ocean water, which helps generate gradually intensifying thunderstorms. When it makes landfall, a hurricane hammers land dwellers with two mighty fists: its howling winds, which have been recorded as gusting over 200 m.p.h., and the strong storm surge it drives before it, which can elevate ocean levels by more than 20 ft., sending floodwaters cascading over beaches, breakwaters and levees. Hurricane Katrina's storm surge in 2005 was so powerful that it picked up a 13,000-ton oil-rig platform from dry dock on the Mobile River in Alabama and carried it upstream, against the river's natural current, then hurled it against a highway bridge, where it came to rest.

Yet all our knowledge of how hurricanes take shape hasn't helped us fight them; man's tools are powerless against such vast weather phenomena. So scientists keep working to improve our ability to predict their movement, in hopes of providing early, accurate warnings to coastal residents. In 1943 a brave pioneer, Major Joseph Duckworth, opened a new era in storm research

HURRICANE HUNTERS

Over the past 25 years, hurricane forecasting has improved significantly, thanks in large part to advances in the technologies used to track the storms

One of eight monitoring stations

HOW HURRICANES FORM . . .

1 A cluster of thunderstorms gather to form a **low-pressure area,** which draws in air and generates **spin** in a counterclockwise direction

2 **Warm ocean water** fuels the transfer of heat and moisture to generate thunderstorms that **rise upward.** If there are no strong winds to break the storm up, it intensifies

3 When wind speeds reach **74 m.p.h. (120 km/h)** or higher and a distinct eye has formed in the center, the storm is called a **hurricane.** When the hurricane moves over cool water or land, it loses energy and weakens

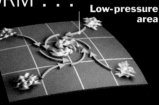

Low-pressure area

Light winds

Warm ocean water

. . . AND HOW THEY ARE TRACKED

The **WP-3D Orion** aircraft flies at 1,500 to 10,000 ft. (400 to 3,000 m) through the hurricane, using a **figure-4 flight path** that allows observation of all **four quadrants** of the storm

The WP-3D has **radar systems** on its nose and under its belly that measure rainfall density to determine the level of turbulence. Doppler radar on the tail records wind speeds

Two types of probes are released: the **dropwindsonde** measures air conditions, and the AXBT plunges into the ocean to record water temperatures

Cool descending air

Warm, moist ascending air

Eye

Heaviest rain and highest wind speeds

Storm surge

Significant hurricane-force winds extend as far as 40 to 100 miles (64 to 161 km) from the eye

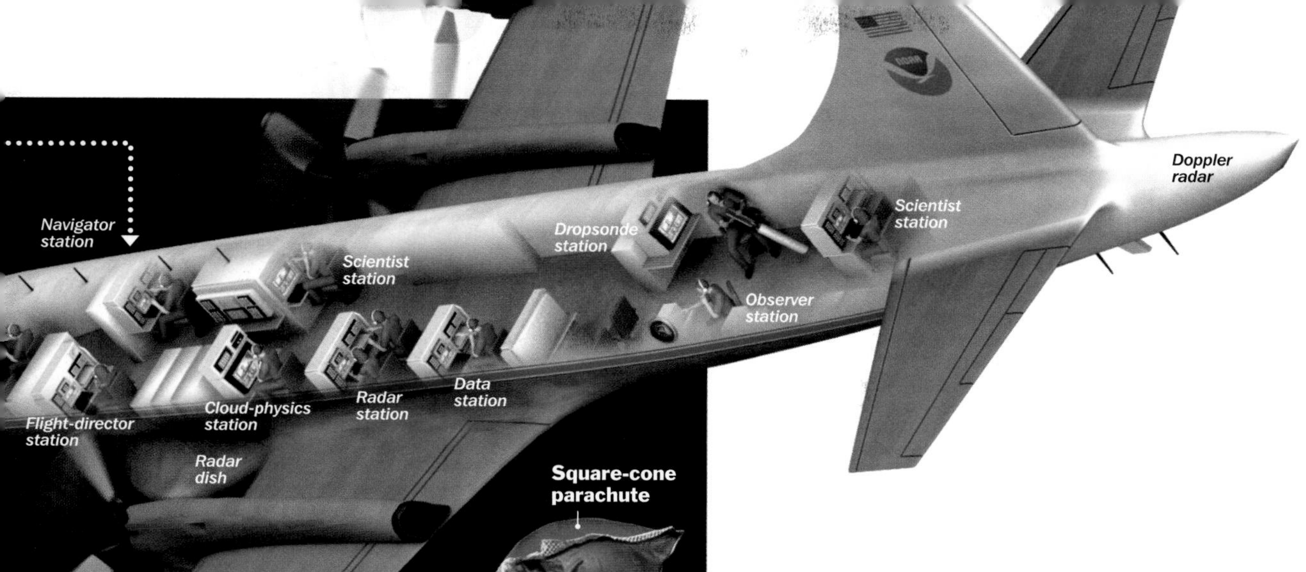

The diagram labels

Navigator station

Scientist station

Dropsonde station

Scientist station

Doppler radar

Observer station

Flight-director station

Cloud-physics station

Radar station

Data station

Radar dish

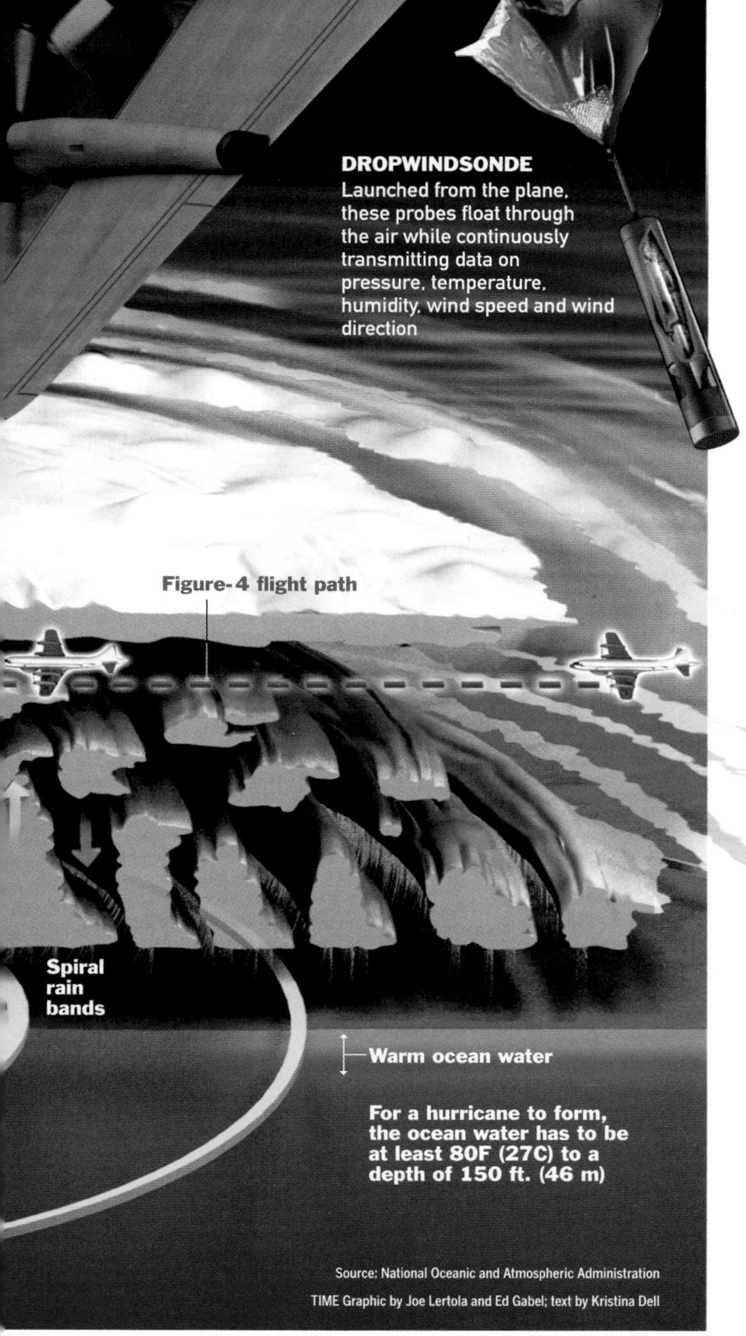

Square-cone parachute

DROPWINDSONDE
Launched from the plane, these probes float through the air while continuously transmitting data on pressure, temperature, humidity, wind speed and wind direction

Figure-4 flight path

Spiral rain bands

Warm ocean water

For a hurricane to form, the ocean water has to be at least 80F (27C) to a depth of 150 ft. (46 m)

Source: National Oceanic and Atmospheric Administration

TIME Graphic by Joe Lertola and Ed Gabel; text by Kristina Dell

when he flew his trainer airplane into a hurricane and returned with valuable readings of the speed and movement of its winds.

Today's weather satellites can capture real-time images of forming hurricanes, but there's no substitute for the close encounters provided by storm-tracking aircraft like the Lockheed WP-3D Orion flown by the National Oceanic and Atmospheric Administration. TIME correspondent J. Madeleine Nash hitched a ride on one such flight in September 2004, as Hurricane Ivan was advancing on the U.S. Gulf Coast. "The plane ... is itself a flying data-collecting instrument," Nash reported, "with an air-sampling rod protruding from its nose and three radar units fastened to its nose, belly and tail. In addition, it has a pipe in the fuselage for launching sensor-loaded canisters known as dropwindsondes, sleek probes that take continuous readings of wind speeds, temperature, pressure and humidity as they parachute down. By combining the data obtained by multiple dropwindsondes, computer models can reconstruct the environment both inside and outside a hurricane, identifying conditions that feed or sap its strength or steer it ... As a result, five-day hurricane-track forecasts are as accurate today as three-day forecasts were 15 years ago."

Ivan was classified a Category 5 storm as it approached the U.S. mainland, but its wind speeds fell from 160 m.p.h. to 130 m.p.h. before it made landfall near Gulf Shores, Ala., on Sept. 16. As Nash noted, thanks to advance warnings, "hundreds of thousands of people fled New Orleans as Ivan approached, removing themselves from the threat of a storm surge in Lake Pontchartrain that could have flooded a city that lies largely below sea level." A year later another hurricane approached the Crescent City, and the warnings went out again. But this time its levees were breached, and a great American metropolis was swamped by Katrina's power—or, if you like, by Katrina's wrath. ■

Hurricanes: A Century of Devastation

GALVESTON, 1900 Striking at the beginning of the 20th century, the greatest natural disaster in U.S. history swamped the island city off the Texas coast on Sept. 8, killing at least 8,000 people and perhaps many more, double the estimated death toll in the San Francisco earthquake and fire of 1906. A massive storm surge driven by the hurricane's winds did much of the damage. The storm was unusually long lived; it wreaked havoc on buildings in Houston, then moved north. On Sept. 11, winds in Chicago were reported at 80 m.p.h.

CAMILLE, 1969 Pursuing a deadly trajectory similar to Katrina's in 2005, Camille smashed up against the Gulf Coast in Mississippi and Louisiana on Aug. 17. Robert Simpson, then head of the National Hurricane Center in Miami, called it "the greatest storm of any kind that has ever affected this nation, by any yardstick you want to measure with." The statement is still valid in 2011. As TIME reported in its Aug. 29, 1969, issue, "Riding waves 22 ft. high, throwing rain hard as bullets on its 210 m.p.h. winds, Camille hurled herself at the Louisiana and Mississippi shoreline, uprooting, ravaging, killing in her awesome kinetic fury. In one fearful night, at least 235 were killed. For a time, the ocean's storm surge reclaimed as much as six blocks of Pass Christian, Gulfport and other hapless Mississippi towns." At left, a yacht fetches up on land in Biloxi, Miss.

ANDREW, 1992 Ravaging a swath of Florida south of Miami in mid-August, with sustained winds of 142 m.p.h., Andrew left some $25 billion in damages. TIME's report at the time seems an eerie forecast of Katrina in 2005: "Armed troops patrolled the streets to stop looters, some of whom brought in rental trucks to haul away their booty. The response by state and federal government was slow and disjointed."

FRANCES, 2004 Floridians will long recall 2004 as "the year of four hurricanes." Over a period of six weeks, a murderer's row of storms took their turns at battering the Sunshine State. Charley struck first, on Aug. 13, smacking into the Gulf Coast 100 miles south of Tampa. Next up was Frances, which made landfall on Sept. 7 as a Category 2 storm just north of Palm Beach, leaving ruined citrus crops in its wake, left. Days later, it was Ivan's turn: the big blow smacked into Florida's Panhandle and the coast of Alabama on Sept. 16. Striking last was Jeanne, which followed Frances' course, landing near Fort Pierce as a Category 3 storm on Sept. 26. More than 400 miles wide, Jeanne tossed debris and churned up floods from Miami to Daytona Beach. Said Governor Jeb Bush: "This is the price we pay, I guess, for living in paradise."

CHARLEY, 2004 The four hurricanes that besieged Florida in 2004 also bred misery on islands across the Caribbean Sea. More than 3,000 people died in Haiti when Hurricane Jeanne caused mudslides. Above, a homeless Xiomara Santamaria weeps while carrying her grandson in Playa Baracoa, outside Havana, on Aug. 13, a day after Charley hit Cuba.

It's a Twister!

When a big thunderstorm spins off a tornado, the results can be deadly

AMERICANS LOVE TO SPIN YARNS, AND when it comes to the weather, some of the best examples of hyperbole involve tornadoes. We've all heard the stories. One twister drove a piece of straw deep inside a thick fence post. Another picked up a woman cowering in her bathtub, carried her and the tub outside, across the yard and right into the woods. Then there's the story about the Kansas farm girl who was picked up by a big twister and carried to a magical land somewhere over the rainbow. Perhaps you're familiar with that one.

Meteorologists love to swap these stories almost as much as they enjoy debunking them. Take the one about tornadoes driving bits of straw through fence posts. What may actually happen, scientists suggest, is that a sudden drop in air pressure forces the wood to expand, allowing pieces of straw to lodge in newly opened cracks. Trouble is, not all the stories are exaggerated: Betty Lou Pearce, then 64, a clerk from Pilot, N.C., was the recipient of that unexpected bathtub sleigh ride in 1996; she returned from her journey bruised but otherwise unharmed.

Across the broad swath of the American heartland known as Tornado Alley, no sight is more feared than a funnel-shaped cloud, no sound less welcome than the wail of a tornado-warning siren piercing the unearthly, portentous calm that often precedes a big twister. Small wonder: with winds that can reach as high as 250 m.p.h., tornadoes are serial killers, striking again and again in Oklahoma, Kansas and Missouri and, less frequently, elsewhere in the nation. The deadliest tornado of 2010 rampaged through Yazoo City, Miss., on April 24, killing 10 people

in the region. On June 5, seven people died when a twister struck Milbury, Ohio, southeast of Toledo. All told, 45 Americans died in tornadoes in 2010. On average, according to the National Oceanic and Atmospheric Administration, 1,000 tornadoes are reported in the U.S. each year, claiming 80 lives and injuring 1,500 people.

What turns a common thunderstorm into a twister? Tornadoes are most often formed by supercell storms, towering cloud structures that can top out at 65,000 ft. and concentrate energy in dangerous ways. A supercell typically takes shape in spring, as warm, moist air from the Gulf of Mexico flows north and pushes through colder, dryer layers of air. As it rises, this upwelling of warm air begins to cool off a bit, and the moisture it contains condenses, first into cloud droplets and then into rain. At that point, the air—now denser because it is colder—starts to sink. But at the same time, the process of condensation that created the rain releases so much latent heat that the air around it warms up once again and retains its lift.

The collision between warm and cold air masses sets up conditions that favor the growth of big thunderstorms. A tornado, however, requires something more: the presence of wind shear, which occurs when winds in the so-called boundary layer—the part of the atmosphere closest to the earth—blow more gently than winds at higher elevations. These two wind streams push on the layer of air that lies between them as though it were an invisible rolling pin. Then, as the warm updraft of a supercell shoots toward the stratosphere, it tilts the rolling pin so that it spins on its end. Soon the entire updraft is spinning, giving birth to a mesocyclone, a rotating column of air as wide as 6 miles. Mesocyclones are the cloud structures from which tightly coiled tornadoes seem to drop; scientists are trying to find out how one turns into the other.

The simplest explanation is that tornadoes form when a smaller, even more rapidly rotating updraft descends from the mesocyclone like a vacuum cleaner nozzle. To our eyes, that is exactly what appears to be happening. But while scientists agree that the updraft is essential,

MIAMI, 1997 *Hurricane-savvy Floridians were startled when a tornado dropped in on May 12; no serious injuries were reported*

OKLAHOMA CITY, 2003 *This factory was leveled by a tornado on May 9; the storm's path of destruction stretched for 35 miles*

many doubt that it provides the sole mechanism for tornado formation. Some think the rapid sinking of colder, dryer air near the rear of the storm may be key. Another possibility: tornadoes may be similar to waterspouts and dust devils, which build their vortices not from the clouds down but from the ground up. It's possible that tornadoes form both ways, top-down and bottom-up.

As with hurricanes, scientists can't control tornadoes; the goal is to predict their appearance and trajectory more accurately. The biggest advance in recent decades is Doppler radar, which takes advantage of radio waves that shift frequency depending on whether the rain droplets they bounce off of are advancing or receding. As the winds inside storm clouds begin to spin, the droplets show up on radar screens as tighter swirls, aiding advance detection of tornado formation—and saving lives.

Collaboration between radar developers and storm chasers led to the Next-Generation Radar system, which the National Weather Service installed nationwide by 1997. The new system has extended the lead time for tornado warnings from 3 to 11 min., on average, saving more lives. If meteorologists keep at it, we soon may know everything there is to know about tornadoes. But that won't stop the unlikely stories from getting spun, and it won't stop the pleasure we get in swapping them. ∎

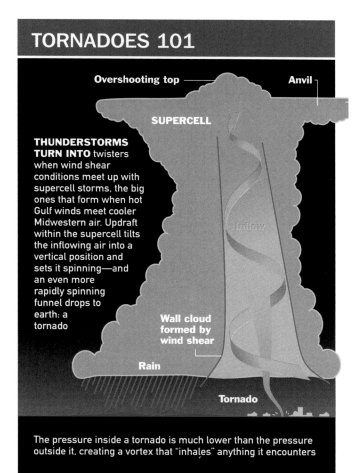

TORNADOES 101

Overshooting top — **Anvil**

SUPERCELL

THUNDERSTORMS TURN INTO twisters when wind shear conditions meet up with supercell storms, the big ones that form when hot Gulf winds meet cooler Midwestern air. Updraft within the supercell tilts the inflowing air into a vertical position and sets it spinning—and an even more rapidly spinning funnel drops to earth: a tornado

Inflow

Wall cloud formed by wind shear

Rain

Tornado

The pressure inside a tornado is much lower than the pressure outside it, creating a vortex that "inhales" anything it encounters

TUCSON, 1990 *A bolt rocks the Arizona city. Scientists are now exploring lightning events that happen above storm clouds, where other electrical discharges occur*

Fatal Splendor

Lightning thrills—and, yes, it kills

LIGHTNING IS NATURE IN ITS MOST DECEPtive guise. It's thrilling, in its way; a dazzling exhibition of nature in all its pyrotechnic power. There's a certain authority to it as well, as a mighty boom follows the flash of light, demanding the atention of your ears in case your eyes missed the show. But lightning is not merely a stirring display: it claims more lives in the U.S. each year, just under 100, than any other natural cause, except for flash floods. Reason: unlike a tsunami or a hurricane, lightning is commonplace. Scientists estimate that lightning bolts strike the ground some 30 million times in the U.S. each year—and there are five times as many bolts that are cloud to cloud.

As for the science involved, comic George Carlin wasn't far off when he said, "Electricity is really just organized lightning." Ben Franklin was the first to prove that lightning is electricity, and you might expect that some 250 years later, scientists would thoroughly understand it, but that's not the case. We know that cloud-to-ground lightning, the dangerous stuff, originates high in the clouds, 15,000 to 20,000 ft. (4.6 to 6 km) above sea level, where raindrops begin to freeze. But we're still not certain how this process results in polarization, the separation of cloud particles into two groups, one charged positively, the other negatively.

We do have a clear picture of what happens next: a lightning strike is actually a two-part process. First, an almost invisible, negatively charged streamer moves toward the ground at blinding speed, descending in 50-yd. sections called step leaders, seeking a positively charged channel to complete its circuit. When it finds such a channel—a tree, a metal rod, a fence post or a human body—a connection is joined, the current soars, and sparks fly. This return stroke, far more luminous than the descending stroke, is the one we see. Inside that glowing bolt, the air is heated to about 50,000°F. When this hot air naturally expands, it forms a shock wave: thunder. And as Mark Twain pointed out, "Thunder is good, thunder is impressive, but it is lightning that does the work." Don't let it do its work on you. ■

Beauty And the Blast

A close encounter with a Near-Earth Object put an end to the long reign of the dinosaurs. Is mankind next?

WILL CIVILIZATION END WITH A whimper? Perhaps, but it seems more and more likely that man's world may go the way of the dinosaurs: with a bang. Most scientists now think that an asteroid smacked into the planet 65 million years ago, leading to the abrupt demise of the dinosaurs and clearing the way for the rise of mammals.

This breakthrough theory was first advanced by physicist Luis Alvarez, the late Nobel laureate, who proposed in 1980 that a giant celestial intruder had triggered the dinosaurs' downfall. The clue that inspired Alvarez was in a thin layer of clay found around the world that forms the so-called K-T boundary between the fossil-rich rock of the Cretaceous period, which ended with the extinctions, and the overlying, younger and sparsely fossiled rock of the Tertiary period. When analysis of the clay revealed that it had a far higher content of the rare element iridium, which is ordinarily found in Earth's crust,

Alvarez proposed that the element might be of extraterrestrial origin. Both comets and asteroids, Alvarez knew, are rich in iridium.

From that evidence, Alvarez constructed this scenario: some 65 million years ago, a comet or asteroid at least five miles (8 km) wide struck Earth and blasted out a tremendous crater. The cosmic interloper was completely obliterated, and a great fireball rose into the stratosphere, carrying with it vast amounts of debris. These finer particles remained suspended and were circulated by air currents until they enshrouded Earth, blocking sunlight for many months, even years. In the ensuing cold and dark, plants and animals perished. When the dust shroud, including the iridium-rich remnants of the comet or asteroid, eventually settled back to Earth, it formed the telltale worldwide layer of clay in the K-T boundary.

Many scientists, particularly paleontologists, initially scoffed at the Alvarez theory. They argued that gradual climatic change, perhaps brought on by heightened vol-

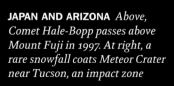

JAPAN AND ARIZONA *Above, Comet Hale-Bopp passes above Mount Fuji in 1997. At right, a rare snowfall coats Meteor Crater near Tucson, an impact zone*

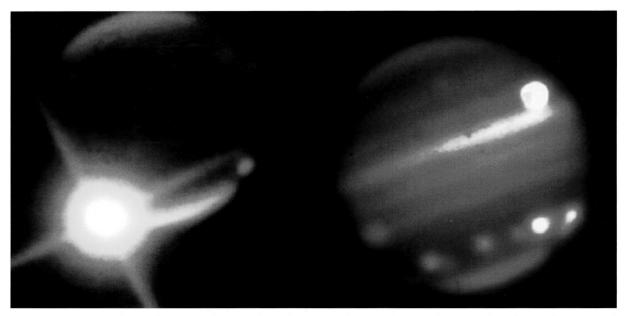

JUPITER, 1994 *Two of the 21 fragments of Comet Shoemaker-Levy 9 plow into the giant planet; similar collisions threaten Earth*

canic activity, had caused the worldwide extinctions. But the discovery in 1990 of a long-hidden crater 112 miles (180 km) in diameter, whose center is below the town of Chicxulub on the northern tip of Mexico's Yucatán peninsula, gave the doubters pause. And the later confirmation of the crater's age—65 million years—led most scientists to jump aboard the Alvarez bandwagon.

Not everyone was convinced. NASA scientists, for example, suggested that most of the airborne dust from the impact explosion and soot from fires ignited in forests would have settled back to the ground within six months, far too soon to have caused extinctions. They offered another explanation, based on the fact that the Yucatán rock around Chicxulub contains heavy amounts of sulfur. The blast must have vaporized the sulfur, they argued, and spewed more than 100 billion tons of it into the atmosphere, where it mixed with moisture to form tiny drops of sulfuric acid. These drops created a barrier that could have reflected enough sunlight back into space to drop temperatures to near freezing, and they could have been airborne for decades.

Other scientists argued for a "double whammy" theory that suggests that an impact on one side of Earth could produce massive volcanic activity at the antipode—a point directly opposite on the far side—and that the combined effect would cause disaster.

The argument over the mechanism by which a comet or asteroid collision might have sparked a massive die-off of plants and animals on our planet may continue for some time. But events in the summer of 1994 turned conjecture into reality. On July 16, the first fragment of Comet Shoe-

maker-Levy 9 plowed into the planet Jupiter with the force of perhaps 10 million hydrogen bombs, lofting a mushroom cloud of hot gas nearly 1,000 miles (1,609 km) into space. After a first bright flash, the impact left dark scars on the planet's surface. Twenty more hits, some larger, followed; the comet had been torn into 21 fragments by Jupiter's dense gravity as it neared the planet. The impacts rival only massive solar flares as the most violent events humans have witnessed in the solar system.

How would such an impact affect Earth, a far smaller planet than Jupiter? If one of Shoemaker-Levy 9's bigger pieces—say a mile or two in diameter—came streaking in at 130,000 m.p.h., it could tear through the atmosphere and smash into the ground with the force of millions of H-bombs, gouging out a crater the size of Rhode Island and throwing so much pulverized real estate into the stratosphere that the sun would be blocked for months while all Earth went into a deep freeze. If the comet were to hit an ocean, a pall of dust would rise from underwater sediment, and a huge megatsunami could race hundreds of miles inland, swamping everything in its path.

Scared? Here's something worse. When it comes to asteroids' wreaking disaster on Earth, the real question may be not if but when. Two hundred or so large craters and a geological record stretching over billions of years provide plenty of evidence that, time and again, impacts with meteors have destroyed large parts of the planet, wiped out species and threatened the very existence of terrestrial life. Scientists term these celestial bodies Near-Earth Objects (NEOs). Astronomers are all too aware that more of them are out there, hurtling through space, some of them ultimately destined to collide with Earth.

A Collision in Siberia

IF THE PROSPECT that a heavenly body might collide with Earth seems a bit far-fetched, think again. The most recent major impact occurred in 1908, in the remote Tunguska region of Russia. Scientists now believe that a meteorite at least 100 ft. (30 m) in diameter exploded some five miles (8 km) above the ground here. Trees in a nine-mile radius from ground zero were incinerated, and some 60 million more were felled.

The region was so remote that the first major scientific expedition did not reach the area until 1927. Investigating geologists found high levels of iridium in the soil—the same clue that was used decades later to correlate the demise of the dinosaurs to a similar collision.

BETTMANN / CORBIS

As recently as 1996, an asteroid about a third of a mile wide passed within 280,000 miles (450,616 km) of Earth, a hairbreadth by astronomical standards. It was the largest object ever observed to pass that close to our home planet. Had it hit, the big rock would have caused an explosion measuring in the 5,000-to-12,000-megaton range. What was particularly unnerving about this flyby is that the asteroid was discovered only four days before it hurtled past Earth.

According to NASA scientists, over the past two decades it has become apparent that Earth lies amid a swarm of small rocky bodies, themselves orbiting the sun, most likely dispatched from the asteroid belt to the inner solar system by the gravitational influence of Jupiter. These bodies vary in size from a few meters to several kilometers. It used to be thought that such objects were rare, much like comets. This view has changed in light of increasingly sensitive surveys by both spacecraft and observatories on land, which have identified an exponentially increasing number of NEOs, many times more than previously believed. Scientists now term these objects PHAs, Potentially Hazardous Asteroids.

In 1999 scientists unveiled a risk-assessment scale to convey the chances of a collision with a given NEO; it was named the Torino scale, after the Italian city in which it was adopted. The scale takes into account the object's size and speed, as well as the probability that it will collide with Earth. On the scale, very close encounters are generally assigned a value of 7 or 8; certain collisions are 9 or 10. Since the system's debut, the closest NEO flyby was labeled a 1—good news, but only in the short run.

What can we do to avoid a collision? Scientists suggest that we might intercept a comet before it hits us, diverting its path. In the first test of our ability to intercept an NEO, a probe released by NASA's Deep Impact spacecraft collided with Comet Tempel 1 on July 4, 2005, producing the same explosive bang as 4.5 tons of TNT. The purpose of the exercise had nothing to do with NEO deflection. Rather, it was to blast a crater into the comet nucleus so that its interior could be studied. Still, it proved that such cosmic targeting was possible—even if it changed Tempel 1's speed by just 0.014 m.p.h. ∎

NORTHERN QUEBEC *Canada's circular Clearwater Lakes, not far from Hudson Bay, are believed to have been formed by a pair of meteorite impacts some 210 million years ago*

Storms on The Sun

Massive solar flares can shut down
power grids, satellites and radio systems

WHEN IT COMES TO BIG STORMS, Planet Earth's hurricanes and tornadoes may be powerful, but they're bush league compared with the sun's periodic flare-ups. Solar flares are twisting arcs of fiery gases, and these eruptions from that great thermonuclear reactor in the sky can stretch as far as the distance from Earth to the moon. The most intense outbursts propel a billion tons of material from the sun's searing (10,000°F) surface at speeds of millions of miles an hour; they are the most violent events we have seen in the solar system. When these electrically charged particles slam against Earth's atmosphere, they can imperil astronauts and push satellites out of orbit— or fry their circuitry. Solar storms reach a peak on roughly an 11-year cycle but can wreak havoc at any time. A huge flare in 1989 blacked out a power grid in Quebec for nine hours, turning out the lights on 6 million people at a cost of more than $30 million. No wonder scientists dream of one day being able to predict storms on the sun with the accuracy of terrestrial weather forecasts.

Solar physicists are drawing ever closer to that goal, thanks to a new generation of solar observatories that have revealed solar processes in fascinating new detail. Since 1996 the NASA–European Space Agency satellite Solar and Heliospheric Observatory has been circling the sun, monitoring its weather and dynamics. A clutch of other satellites followed; most recently, on Feb. 11, 2010, NASA launched the Solar Dynamics Observatory (SDO) into orbit. The most advanced spacecraft ever designed to study the nearest star, the SDO will examine the sun's magnetic field and explore the role the sun plays in Earth's atmosphere and climate. It may also confirm a belief that is growing among scientists: the sun is more variable and dynamic than we had earlier believed.

These new tools have helped us chart a host of solar weather patterns, including an astonishing doughnut-shaped jet stream of hot gases that circles the sun's "arctic" region, like Earth's own circumpolar winds. They've also offered close-up views of the sun's lower-latitude trade winds, confirming that the winds—actually, great bands of superhot plasma—dive deep into the solar interior, itself a mass of gases, then flow back toward the equator, creating a gyre reminiscent of Earth's great ocean currents. The hope: by learning to forecast solar weather, we can plan in advance for solar flares. ■

SURFACE OF THE SUN *This image from a solar-tracking satellite shows a relatively quiet day on the sun in September 2000; these flares are far smaller than the ones during storms*